Twayne's English Authors Series

Sylvia E. Bowman, *Editor*

INDIANA UNIVERSITY

Nevil Shute

TEAS 190

Nevil Shute

NEVIL SHUTE
(NEVIL SHUTE NORWAY)

By JULIAN SMITH

San Diego State University

TWAYNE PUBLISHERS
A DIVISION OF G. K. HALL & CO., BOSTON

Library of Congress Cataloging in Publication Data

Smith, Julian, 1937-
   Nevil Shute (Nevil Shute Norway)

   (Twayne's English authors series ; TEAS 190)
   Bibliography: p. 159 - 61.
   Includes index.
   1. Norway, Nevil Shute, 1899-1960.   I.   Title.
PR6027.054Z9   823'.9'12   [B]   76-8018
ISBN 0-8161-6664-2

For Monica

Contents

About the Author

Born in New Orleans, Julian Smith studied at Tulane University and Columbia, where he was a Woodrow Wilson Fellow. Married and the father of three children, he has taught at Georgetown, the University of New Hampshire, Ithaca College, and San Diego State University.

In addition to articles in the popular press, he has published *Looking Away: Hollywood and Vietnam* (Charles Scribner's Sons, 1975) and about thirty scholarly or critical pieces in such journals as *American Literature, American Quarterly, Arizona Quarterly, Connecticut Review, Film Quarterly, Journal of Modern Literature, Journal of Popular Film, Literature/Film Quarterly, Nineteenth Century Fiction, The Personalist, South Atlantic Quarterly, Studies in Short Fiction, Twentieth Century Literature,* and elsewhere.

This study of Nevil Shute was written with the aid of a grant from the National Endowment for the Humanities.

Preface

Most critical biographies of modern writers tend to give emphasis to the writer's literary surroundings. Nevil Shute presents a special problem in that he knew and read few other writers; moreover, apart from a fondness for certain poets and adventure writers whom he read as a young man, he had absolutely no interest in literature. Worse, from the point of view of the psychologically oriented critic, he led a dreadfully respectable, monogamous, and frequently monotonous life. He was, to put it mildly, all business. At first his chief business was engineering, then industrial management, then war; but during all this time, his main interest was writing.

The most important influence on Shute as a man and as a writer seems to have been his training and his early life as an engineer. Like the lawyer or physician who turns to literature, he never forsook the habits of thought bred into him as a young man; and he was, above all, a practical businessman. When asked if he thought he would have been so tremendously successful as a novelist had he not had long experience in industry, he replied: "I think not. What the literary people in the ivory towers forget is that business is the key to everything — to the good life, to the arts, to civilization itself."[1] Whatever psychic or emotional maladjustments Shute may have suffered do not appear in his fiction; and standard psychological concerns of modern writers do not appear there either: no father-son conflicts; few recognizable rites of passage; no preoccupation with abstractions like fate or evil. There is much love in his fiction, but little passion.

Yet his life is important, and for that reason I have organized this book chronologically to show the relationship between his life and his fiction. Though none of his novels is explicitly autobiographical, all of his books come directly out of his life, his work, his times, his environment, and his interests in a way that is seldom observable in other writers. "I'm a person with a succession of short-lived enthusiasms," he said late in his life. "I get worked up about something like the possibility of atomic war, eastern religion or Britain's political position, and then begin wondering what sort of people would get involved in such situations. From that emerges a story."[2] To a very real extent, Nevil Shute lived in his books — thus, I have tried to show the development and consistency of one writer whose published works span almost forty years.

Because this is the first full-length study of Nevil Shute, I have incurred many debts. Thus, I wish to express my appreciation to the following: to the Estate of Nevil Shute Norway for permission to quote from his unpublished works; to his Estate, to R. P. Watt and Sons, his literary agents, and to his publishers, William Heinemann, Ltd., and William Morrow and Company, for permission to quote from his published works; to his publishers for allowing me to examine their correspondence and editorial files; to the libraries of the University of New Hampshire, Ithaca College, and Cornell University, and especially to the National Library of Australia and to the George Arents Research Library of Syracuse University and to its former Director of Special Collections, Dr. Howard Applegate; to the National Endowment for the Humanities for the travel and research grant that made it possible for me to go to England and Australia in search of Nevil Shute; to the many friends of Nevil Shute who helped me in my study, and especially to Mrs. Sally Bessant, his secretary, to the late Frances Mary Norway, his widow, and to his daughters, Shirley Norway and Heather Norway Mayfield, for their many kindnesses; to Mrs. Dorothy Owens for typing the manuscript for this book — and to my wife and children for their patience.

JULIAN SMITH

San Diego State University

Chronology

1899	Nevil Shute Norway born January 17 in Ealing, a suburb of London.
1910	Plays truant from school for ten days in Science Museum and is sent to the Dragon School in Oxford.
1912	His father, a senior civil servant, becomes head of post office in Ireland; family moves to Dublin.
1913 - 1916	At Shrewsbury School in Oxford. Spends vacations in countryside near Dublin.
1915	Only brother, age nineteen, dies in France.
1916	Serves as a stretcher bearer in Easter Rebellion; father's post office occupied by rebels and burned.
1917 - 1918	Trains at Royal Military Academy as Royal Flying Corps gunnery officer, but fails final medical examination because of stammer; enlists in the infantry, but Armistice keeps him from combat.
1919 - 1922	At Balliol College, Oxford. Spends holidays yachting and working at the de Havilland Aircraft Company.
1923	Joins de Havillands as a full-time stress and performance calculator; learns to fly; writes and soon shelves first novel, "Stephen Morris," about a young aeronautical engineer just down from Oxford.
1924	Leaves de Havillands to join R.100 airship project on which he works for next six years as chief calculator; writes and shelves "Pilotage," a continuation of "Stephen Morris."
1926	As "Nevil Shute," publishes *Marazan*.
1928	Publishes *So Disdained;* becomes Deputy Chief Engineer of the airship project and stops writing.
1930	Flies to Canada and back in R.100; disastrous crash of rival F.101 ends airship project. Out of work, helps found a new company to build planes, Airspeed Ltd.

1931   Marries Frances Heaton; becomes joint managing director of Airspeed; finishes *Lonely Road* in early summer and stops writing to devote energies to growing firm.

1934   Elected Fellow of Royal Aeronautical Society.

1937   Starts writing again after *Lonely Road* is filmed.

1938   Resigns from Airspeed Ltd.; publishes *Ruined City* and sells film rights; turns full-time to writing.

1939   Angered by faulty air-raid precautions, writes *What Happened to the Corbetts;* criticizes American isolation in a New York speech; goes to work on development of experimental weapons.

1940   Publishes *An Old Captivity* and *Landfall;* sends wife and two small daughters to Canada; joins British Navy and is assigned to Admiralty Department of Miscellaneous Weapon Development where he remains until 1944 as head of engineering section.

1941   Promoted to Lieutenant Commander; writes *Pied Piper,* which is filmed the following year.

1942   Writes *Most Secret,* but novel withheld from publication by Admiralty censors for security reasons.

1943   Admiralty duties keep him from writing.

1944   Writes *Pastoral*; goes to Normandy with invasion fleet as correspondent for Ministry of Information.

1945   Resigns from navy; writes *Vinland the Good*; goes to Burma as correspondent; publishes *Most Secret*; begins *The Chequer Board,* inspired largely by Burma trip.

1947   Publishes *The Chequer Board*; travels by car through America.

1948   Publishes *No Highway,* an aeronautical engineering novel; writes most of another novel, then abandons it.

1948 - September to March, flies his own plane to Australia and
1949   back in search of material for new books.

1949   As a result of Australian trip, writes *A Town Like Alice* and begins *Round the Bend.*

1950   Finishes *Round the Bend*; moves to Australia in July.

1951   Writes *The Far Country*; has heart attack and stops flying; begins thinking about autobiography.

1952   Writes *In the Wet* to forecast future of British Commonwealth.

1953   Writes *Slide Rule,* his autobiography up to 1938; begins *Requiem for a Wren.*

Chronology

1954   Explores Australian oil fields by station wagon and American Rockies by packhorse.

1955   Trip of year before results in *Beyond the Black Stump*; minor heart attack in November.

1956   Buys Jaguar, takes up sportscar racing, and writes *On the Beach*.

1957   Writes *The Rainbow and the Rose*.

1958   Travels extensively; filming of *On the Beach* begins near his home; has major stroke in December soon after beginning *Trustee from the Toolroom*.

1959   Despite a second stroke in May, finishes *Trustee* and sends a memorandum to Prime Minister Menzies about economic condition of artists in Australia; begins mystical "Incident at Eucla" in November.

1960   January 12, death of Shute.

CHAPTER 1

A Child of the Century

I The Early Years

NEVIL Shute was not trained as a writer, nor did he have any early intentions of becoming one. What he wanted most as a boy was to "mess around" with machines. Born with aviation in 1899, he spent his formative years in a house directly between two of London's earliest aerodromes. A bad stammer and a worse schoolmaster caused him to play truant for ten days in London's Science Museum where he forgot his loneliness and guilt in studying real locomotives, motorcars, and planes. Discovered and placed in another school, he was happier, especially because he could watch the young masters tinkering with their motorbikes and a young mechanic named Morris building motorcars to order in his small garage. Finally, when Shute was fifteen, he obtained his first machine, a motorcycle. These are typical of the facts and incidents he chose to emphasize in his autobiography.

Born in suburban Ealing, west of London on the edge of farming land, Shute enjoyed a fairly ordinary upper-middle-class childhood and youth. His mother was the daughter of a major general in the Indian Army; his father, forty years older than Nevil, was a senior civil servant in the General Post Office in London until he became head of the postal service in Ireland. In 1912, the family moved to a country house near Dublin where Nevil and his older brother Fred spent idyllic summers in the Irish country; the rest of the time, he was away at Shrewsbury School. The Edwardian calm was broken by World War I. Fred was killed in France; and young Nevil served as an ambulance attendant during the Easter Rebellion when his father's post office was occupied by the rebels and burned. In 1917, he entered the Royal Military Academy and spent nine months contentedly training as a Flying Corps gunner; but he failed the precommissioning medical examination because of his stammer.

After three months' treatment for the stammer, he failed to get a commission in the Royal Air Force; and, desperate to get into action, he ended up enlisting in the infantry in August, 1918, only a few months before the Armistice.

The closest Shute came to the carnage of the war was as a member of a permanent funeral party that conducted military funerals for victims of the influenza epidemic that struck at the end of the war. "The Dead March still brings back memories to me of pleasant excursions through Kent by train or truck, freed from the pressure of military training and with a new, unknown, and glamorous world opening before me" (*Slide Rule*, 32).[1] This passage from his autobiography not only exemplifies his early stoicism, but his ability to take pleasure in the variety of life. Moreover, this appreciation and almost total *acceptance* of the world enabled him to write two dozen books that reached millions of readers.

Demobilized, Shute entered Oxford where, in his own words, he was "a very ordinary, humdrum undergraduate. I excelled at nothing, won one prize only, which I spent upon a set of drawing instruments and a copy of *The Earthly Paradise* by William Morris . . . and took third class honours in Engineering" (*Slide Rule*, 34). Engineering and William Morris were an odd combination on the surface, but a revealing one that reminds us of an earlier assurance that science would indeed create an earthly paradise. Unlike that other Oxonian, Aldous Huxley, who was suspicious of what technology would do, Shute embarked hopefully upon the new era.

All through his college years he had written what he later considered very bad poetry; and all through his mature years he would read poetry and quote it extensively in epigraphs, chapter headings, and titles (*On the Beach*, for instance, comes from T. S. Eliot). He analyzed his failure as a poet in *Slide Rule* in mechanical terms appropriate to an engineer: "First I wrote poetry, probably because a poem is the shortest complete work that is possible, and being entirely emotional it requires little experience of life. Moreover, you don't have to have a typewriter to write a poem. What I didn't realize, of course, is that a piece of writing is like a camera; the smaller it is the more carefully it has to be made. In a novel a few awkward passages can get lost in the crowd, but in a short poem every word must play its part and be exactly right" (47).

What probably kept Shute from writing at greater length was the lack of *digested* experience — a factor understandable in a young man who had been shuttled from school to army to university and who had not been given the time to devote to a major interest. The turning point for the budding engineer and novelist was rapidly approaching; for, having spent most of his college vacations working without pay for the new aircraft company founded by Captain Geoffrey de Havilland, he joined the firm upon graduation from Balliol in January, 1923, as a junior stress and performance calculator. And with his earnings as an engineer, five pounds a week, he did two important things: he learned to fly, and he bought a new typewriter. The first would consummate his love affair with flying machines and give him the subject matter of his earliest and much of his best fiction, aviation; the second, the typewriter, would make it physically possible for him to write quickly in his spare time.

Everything in those early years went well for him: he enjoyed his work, and he gained practical experience quickly. More important, he was in a good position to learn the craft of writing. Unmarried, without formal responsibility beyond his initially simple work, and living only a few yards from the aerodrome so he lost no time in travel, he was able to spend several evenings a week writing. More than his physical advantage was his psychological preparation for writing:

I don't think there is a great deal in the theory that writing ability is dictated by heredity, but I think there is a great deal in environment. My father and my grandmother both wrote a number of books, so that the business was familiar to me before I started. I knew before putting my first finger to the typewriter that what I was about to write would probably be useless and unpublishable through inexperience, because everybody has to learn his trade and the trade of a writer can only be learned by writing. Apart from writing I was getting on well in a good job as an engineer; there was no economic compulsion on me to hawk my stuff around and try to sell it in order to live. (*Slide Rule*, 51 - 52)

A few months before he died, Shute argued, in a memorandum about the economic condition of writers and artists in Australia, that young writers should not be assisted with subsidies in any way:

To write a book is a very easy matter for the man or woman who really wants to do so. No training is necessary. . . . It is better for the young man or woman who wishes to write to take a job in some commercial occupation and to write in the evenings till the writing becomes more profitable. . . . This commercial occupation should have nothing to do with writing, because one cannot turn with enthusiasm to writing in the evening when one has been doing it all day. . . . He is more likely to develop into a dedicated writer if he spends the first ten or fifteen years of his working life in an accountant's office or a bank, in a government office, or in medicine. If then it proves that he has no capacity to earn a living as a writer, he has a solid job behind him to ensure his future.[2]

That Nevil Shute wrote half a dozen books before he became a professional writer might be explained by his birth in a time and in a place in which an educated man was expected to be literate but not to be a "writer." Arthur Hamilton Norway, his civil-servant father, published several travel books, a study of *The Divine Comedy*, and a history of the postal-packet service in which his Cornwall ancestors had been prominent; his grandmother wrote children's books; and his mother produced a volume of letters dealing with the family's experiences in the Sinn Fein Rebellion. Thus, it should not be surprising that young Nevil started writing stories and novels soon after Oxford; what is surprising is that he wrote so much that was at first unpublishable and that, when he did start publishing, he was not deterred by his initial lack of financial or critical success.

A combination of events and influences seems to have driven him to write: the Easter Rebellion, the Great War, his involvement in an exciting new industry. But there were thousands with similar backgrounds who did not feel compelled to write. What made Shute different, I think, was the combination of a basically isolated personality (he was both shy and highly self-sufficient); an extreme reliance on imagination; and a strong desire to create order out of chaos. His was a spirit possessed not by love or hate, by drink or drugs, or even by a passion for writing, but by order and regularity. Any man who titles his autobiography *Slide Rule* and plans a continuation entitled "Set Square" reveals himself an obedient child of the century that made machines both art forms and objects of worship. In a confused and confusing world in which men did not always act as they should, fiction gave Nevil Shute a chance to design and construct ideal human relationships and responses.

II   *The First Novels*

In June, 1923, within six months of starting work with de Havillands, Shute sent his first novel, "Stephen Morris," to a publisher. After three refusals, he put it aside and started "Pilotage," which he wrote in fourteen weeks in early 1924.[3] This manuscript was turned down by at least six publishers and was likewise shelved.

Though Shute spoke of them in his autobiography as very bad jobs, they were published after his death as one volume under the joint title *Stephen Morris* and were made readable through the simple expedient of eliminating juvenile philosophizing and the lengthy opening sections that had postponed the main action.

These two novels are worth examining in detail because they show the beginnings of an extremely competent writer. More important, they indicate his overriding interest in practical matters and in promoting British aviation. The marginally autobiographical "Stephen Morris" deals with a young engineer just down from Oxford who ends up working for a struggling aircraft builder and who proposes to the girl of his dreams. "Pilotage" continues Stephen Morris' story but shifts to a new central character, Peter Dennison, who serves as Morris' navigator on a flying boat experiment to test the feasibility of opening airmail service between London and New York. Written long before the advent of such mail service, "Pilotage" shows the talent for prophecy and speculation that was to mark many of Shute's aviation novels.

Shute's letters to the publishers, neatly filed away with their polite letters of rejection, show that he was concerned about quick publication for both novels — this was to be a concern through much of his career as he usually tried to be extremely fresh in his subject matter, sometimes to the extent of setting his stories in the future. One letter shows he had already developed a practical credo: "In writing ["Stephen Morris"] I had in mind a series of novels, of which this was to be the first, illustrating the growth of Commercial Aviation — a subject upon which I am qualified to write. Each novel was to be complete in itself. To the uninitiated this subject is of little interest; I hoped to be able to infuse a little of the enthusiasm of the aerodrome in to my book."[4]

Although Shute was writing about his own time, he seems to have been prophetic enough to hit upon those aspects of aviation that would soon pass away. With a sure talent for myth-making, he throws Morris into aviation in a period of transition when it "had ceased to attract as a novelty and was not yet accepted as a serious means of transport" (58). In this primitive period, aviation is still a seasonal industry. It is a period of innocence in which the first person Morris encounters in an aircraft firm is a little girl eating an apple.

That his first job amounts to flying sightseers does not bother Morris, for "Surely this aviation would be a great thing, would take the place in the world to which it was entitled . . . before so very long

. . . he would be there to do his bit in the development of this new industry. . . . There would be big fortunes to be made by men who
pinned their faith to it now; one day he might be a rich man. Money
meant such a lot — one could do nothing without money" (20).
From beginning to end, Shute and his characters were never shy
about making money, for money is the surest sign that a man is doing what the world wants done. There was a strong brand of secular
Calvinism in Shute: the world was his god and it was to be served,
and the man who served it well would be amply rewarded.

More than that, the risking of money is the surest sign of faith one
can give in Shute's theology. Thus, there is considerable bitterness in
"Stephen Morris" that the English government has not sufficiently
backed civil aviation — this failure is presented dramatically
through the story of Malcolm Riley, Morris' friend, who undertakes
to fly a fast but dangerous English plane in a European air race just
so England will be represented. Riley crashes before he can even get
to the race, killed by Shute's desire to drive his point home:

It ought to have succeeded, this little venture. It was a generous thing — but
even generous things may come to failure. It failed, principally through lack
of time for the proper preparation of the machine, as so many enterprises in
aviation have failed. . . . If we attempt to follow the cause of this little disaster back still further we quickly get beyond our depth in a morass of
arguments hinging on the lack of money to enter a machine properly, the
poverty of the British aircraft industry, the defense of the Empire, and the
payment of the American debt. The pound goes up in New York — an
aeroplane comes down in Kent. (100 - 101)

Significantly, even the novel's happy ending is tainted by the fact
that Morris' success comes through a contract to build fighter
planes for Denmark, not England.

"Well," said Morris sourly, "we must hope the government won't
risk a war with Denmark. I don't believe any of our machines would stand
a dog's chance against the fighter."

"I know," said Rawdon [Morris' employer and the plane's designer].

Morris glanced with sudden sympathy at the other, somehow rather a
dejected figure despite the contract.

"It's pretty rotten," he said.

"One oughtn't let these things count, of course," said the designer evenly.
"But — oh, it's heartbreaking. I never thought we should come down
to this. . . ." (137)

III *The Writer as Lobbyist*

In "Pilotage," the sequel to "Stephen Morris," Shute went farther down the road to learning his craft. Having eliminated much of the discursiveness and having tightened the cast of characters and the action, he developed thematically the close relationship between aerial and nautical prowess suggested by the title: "Pilotage." One purpose of the novel was to project England's traditional supremacy on the sea into the air. Since England had long been a country of great amateur sailors, Shute built this novel around Peter Dennison, a lawyer who goes sailing and is run down by the yacht of Sir David Fisher, who is backing Stephen Morris and his employer Captain Rawdon in a scheme to provide regular airmail service between London and New York. Dennison, known in yachting circles for his helmsmanship, is signed on as navigator for the flying boat to be piloted by Morris. The experimental flight, the chief action and interest of the book, succeeds; Morris and Rawdon are to proceed with their transatlantic scheme; and Dennison is to work in the legal department of Sir David's shipping line so he will be free to sail his new employer's yacht during the summers.

At times, it is hard to tell which element most interests Shute: air or sea. The point is that the two are linked; that the shipping magnate, Fisher, has a responsibility to invest in civil aviation; that the air industry needs the talents of nautical types like Dennison. Throughout Shute's life and his fiction, he remained attracted equally to air and sea. Though he had spent most of his college holidays working for Geoffrey de Havilland, the prototype of Rawdon, he had also spent two summers (1919 and 1920) helping a retired solicitor sail his yacht; and, even when he was successful enough to own a private airplane, Shute did considerable cruising and in World War II he joined the navy, not the air force. A good part of *Marazan*, his first published novel, is set aboard a pilot's sailboat; *Lonely Road* is about the owner of a small shipping line (whose brother-in-law, a famous pilot, has flown around the world in a flying boat, "an achievement only comparable with that of his progenitor, Sir Francis Drake"); *Ruined City* deals with a financier who reopens a shipyard; in *What Happened to the Corbetts*, a family escapes from aerial bombardment by going to sea — and picks up the crew of a downed plane; *An Old Captivity* parallels an air journey from Europe to the New World with a Viking voyage; *Landfall*, taking its title from seafaring, is about a bomber pilot on sea patrol; *Most Secret* is a novel of sea war; *On the Beach* is about, among other things, the world's last sea voyage; and *Trustee from the Toolroom*, Shute's last novel, contains an almost epic voyage in a small sailboat. In addition, several unpublished manuscripts deal with the sea, most notably "In the Uttermost Parts of the Sea," a novella about an aircraft carrier.

Now, it may be tempting to conclude that Shute was just an overgrown Arthur Ransome, writing saleable adventure stories — but such a conclusion ignores the fact that he did not rely on writing as a living until after World War II, by which time he had published over a dozen novels; and, more important, such a conclusion ignores his practical, serious nature and his almost missionary zeal concerning British aviation. We must remember that Shute came of age in both the early years of aviation and the late years of Britain's greatness. Not long before his birth, the *Encyclopaedia Britannica* article about flight ended with this chauvinistic appeal: "The unremitting efforts of Mr Moy and other British engineers to construct flying machines deserve well of science. They are significant as showing that the great subject of aerial navigation is at length receiving a fair share of the thought and energy of a country which has already produced the steamboat and locomotive, and which, there is good reason to believe, is destined also to produce the flying machine."[5] Nevil Shute's mission throughout the 1920s and 1930s was to build aircraft during the day and to harangue the government and the public at night through his fiction by calmly exposing and dramatizing the shortsighted policies that were allowing Britain to become a second-rate air power.

Nor was his concern solely with defense or England's scientific reputation; rather, he was helping foster the concept of the world as a global village. In "Pilotage," his creature Stephen Morris speaks for him: " 'It seems to me that communications are the whole keynote of present-day politics. One has means for limited rapid communication already, of course, by wireless and cable. But think what it would mean if one could carry bulky documents rapidly. Or people. Think what it would have meant if in August 1914 we could have had every Dominion Prime Minister in London within a week. By air' " (222 - 23).

To be sure, Shute was not alone in his concern. His pilot friend, Alan Cobham, who also worked for de Havillands in the early 1920s and who was later associated with the company Shute started, wrote several accounts of his air travels full of such trumpet calls as this one: "It is vital to the safety of the nation that Britain should become a nation of aviators. In matters of defense, we live on an island no longer. The day that Blériot flew the Channel marked the end of our insular safety, and the beginning of the time when Britain must seek another form of defense besides its ships."[6] But Shute was unique among others in his profession because he was well on his way to becoming a practicing novelist.

CHAPTER 2

The Airship Venture

I The R.100

IF young writer Shute was working at a great pace, turning out two novels in less than a year and a half, the young engineer was working even faster. At about the time he shelved "Pilotage" in the fall of 1924, he left de Havillands, where advancement promised to be slow, to become chief calculator for the R.100, a giant rigid airship being built by a private firm in competition with the air ministry's own airship, the R.101. This project was probably made doubly interesting for the highly logical and sharp-tongued young writer by the fact that the team of government engineers and bureaucrats responsible for designing the R.101 was the same one that had designed the ill-fated R.38 which had killed forty-four men when it broke apart during trials. Most of the R.101's designers and backers were aboard when she crashed on her first long flight with an even greater loss of life; on the other hand, Shute's ship, the R.100, flew to Canada and back without incident.

The six years Shute spent on the R.100 project, from 1924 until 1930 when the R.101 disaster ended airship development in England, gave him great experience and responsibility for both money and lives. More important, they increased his respect for private enterprise and his dislike of bureaucracy — prejudices that became significant in his mature fiction. The R.101 disaster was a central event in his life — he gives it a great portion of his autobiography, and friends say he frequently referred to it. This is not surprising since Shute, with his extremely moral upbringing, was a believer in poetic justice. As a modern man, he must have found a modern moral in the disaster: two teams built airships; the private team, working in competition with the government agency that supervised the competition and set the requirements, worked under terrific disadvantages but had the singular advantage of

24

having to succeed in order to show a profit. And succeeding meant building a machine that worked. The other team, with far more money at its disposal and led by men with much face to save, made mistakes that could not have been tolerated by the cost-conscious private team.[1]

II *Enter "Nevil Shute"*: Marazan

Perhaps the exactness of Shute's work as chief calculator was responsible for the care he put into his next novel, *Marazan*, which he claims to have written and rewritten three times during the eighteen months of planning prior to the start of the actual construction of the R.100. Examination of his mature manuscripts shows he usually took less than six months to finish a novel, writing and then correcting only one draft, except for generally rewriting the first chapter. For young Shute, engineering work was not something that took him away from writing; instead, writing was a relaxation that made it possible for him to forget his work in the evenings and return with a clear head in the morning.

Much later he was to say that, "If I had known that a future as an author awaited me I suppose I should have given up engineering at an early stage, and my life would certainly have been the poorer for it" (*Slide Rule*, 62). Since *Marazan* barely earned its author thirty pounds before it went out of print, little temptation existed for him to quit his first calling. Indeed, the overriding importance of the airship work to him is documented in his decision to publish *Marazan* under his first and middle names for fear his employers "would probably take a poor view of an employee who wrote novels on the side; hard-bitten professional engineers might well consider such a man to be not a serious person" (*Slide Rule*, 63).

Apparently the intention of writing a series of novels dealing with civil aviation was still in his mind when he wrote *Marazan*, for the central character, Philip Stenning, was a minor character in "Stephen Morris"; Stephen Morris himself appears several times in this novel as Stenning's rather dour superior at the Rawdon Air Taxi Service. Stenning, in turn, appears later in *So Disdained* (1928); and, as Sir Philip Stenning, he figures importantly in *Lonely Road* (1932). Stenning seems largely based on Alan Cobham, who at about the time of *Marazan*'s composition was flying to Australia and back, for which feat he was knighted. Like Sir Alan Cobham, Stenning is a walking, talking, flying symbol of British civil aviation after World War I: both are Royal Air Force veterans who fly sightseers, do air

photography work, join passenger airlines, and eventually earn
knighthood for long-distance flights. But the Stenning of *Marazan* is
none too respectable a citizen: the son of a naval officer and a chorus
girl, he is a hard-drinking, socially ambiguous figure who sees
himself in Rudyard Kipling's terms as one of "the sons of Martha":

It is their care in all the ages to take the buffet and cushion the shock,
It is their care that the gear engages, it is their care that the switches lock.[2]

When a friend is murdered by the henchmen of Rodrigo Mattani,
a dope-smuggling supporter of Il Duce, Stenning goes to Italy to
avenge him. Stenning's motive, revenge, is reinforced by his fear
that the innocence and the beauty of England are being destroyed
by a "foreign" criminal. He resolves to destroy Mattani when, looking at a water-color landscape on a calendar, he suddenly notices this
pious little couplet by Kipling:

Our England is a garden, and such gardens are not made
By saying, "Oh, how beautiful!" and sitting in the shade. (147)

Again and again, Shute reduced complex decisions to such
dramatically simple causes. In a complex, chaotic world, he soothed
readers with easily understood motives; then he had his characters
plunge ahead with strenuous overreaching actions.

After some snooping in Florence, where Stenning learns Mattani
is smuggling with the aid of a seaplane, Stenning sets up a trap to
help the police; and, in one of the earliest examples of aerial
mayhem in fiction, he kills Mattani by flying into him as he stands
on the ground shooting at Stenning's plane. This action *sounds*,
in summary, like so much romantic claptrap; and Shute had
obviously read and admired John Buchan and such classic adventures as *The Thirty-nine Steps*. Yet Shute is his own creature, and
Marazan contains some highly personal touches.

Marazan is still a rattling good yarn — but what made it
publishable when Shute's first two novels were not? For one, the
love theme is more fully developed with a heroine who takes an
active part in the plot. Whereas the romantic interest in the first two
novels was limited to providing the protagonist with a conventional
motive for economic success (an income sufficient for marriage), the
heroine in *Marazan* is the prototype of Shute's many adventurous
young women. The flying theme was novel and contemporary, and

the title was exotic yet close to home — Marazan Sound is off the coast of Cornwall. Stylistically, Shute improved his narrative by switching from the third person, which tempted him to pontificate and philosophize, to Stenning's earthy and practical first-person voice. Finally, the first two novels were too "autobiographical" in the sense that Morris strongly resembled Shute in character. By switching to Stenning, who quite rightly finds Morris a bore, Shute had a chance to develop a more interesting central character.

The change in subject can be explained, I think, in terms of Shute's switch from a fairly minor job at de Havillands to an important post on a major new undertaking. At de Havillands, Shute wrote two novels about the kind of work he did — but as one involved with the airship project and as a managing director later of another firm, he was in too sensitive a position to write about his own work. Then too, he probably found airships a poor subject for fiction, largely because there was little opportunity for displaying the individualism found in the other branches of aviation — one man could design, build, and fly the early airplanes; but airships were huge cooperative enterprises. These factors, combined with the desire to be read, turned him away from close attention to his own industry and attracted him in *Marazan* and in his two succeeding novels, *So Disdained* and *Lonely Road*, to the espionage and detective adventure epitomized by John Buchan.

Although Shute was much later to be apologetic about his use of police and spy themes,[3] he need not have been, for not only did Graham Greene, another Heinemann author, get his start in the same way, but their early espionage fiction reflects the sinister and sordid atmosphere of England after World War I. Indeed, espionage in the ensuing years was to become a major genre in British literature. It would seem only natural for the literature of a small country beset by political and social ills to turn to themes of danger, betrayal, and moral ambiguity.

III So Disdained

In these years Shute was leading a life entirely devoted to aviation: during the day, he worked on the airship which was being assembled in a tremendous hanger in Howden; for relaxation, he wrote novels about flying and flew a small plane at the Yorkshire Aeroplane Club which he helped found and where he first met his wife. But the airship work chiefly occupied his mind, for the building of the R.100 was not only a difficult task but one that gave

Shute and his colleagues a massive inferiority complex because of their competition with the air ministry's R.101. The air ministry had more money, it had its own public relations department, and it seemed to be making stupid errors — or were they errors? Shute's team had calculated an airship could be steered by hand, yet the government team had installed heavy servo motors to turn the rudders; the R.100 could be moved astern by reversing the direction of two of the propellors; yet the R.101 designers had ignored the simple method of reversing propellors and had turned one of the massive engines around entirely, thus rendering it useless except for a few minutes at the start and end of each flight. The "capitalist" crew was left incredulous: "It is the greatest mistake to underrate your competitor, and in spite of their past record it was incredible to us that our competitors should perpetrate such childish follies. There *must* be something in this that we did not understand" (*Slide Rule*, 72).

In this atmosphere of doubt and confusion, Shute spent two years writing and rewriting *So Disdained* (1928), a novel reflecting his love of England and of aviation as well as his bitterness at what England was doing to her pilots. While *Marazan* showed the marginal social condition of a pilot as it contrasted with the talents and skills he possessed, it did not seem to be the intentionally propagandistic novel that his first two unpublished efforts had been. But the social and economic condition of the pilot in *So Disdained* is shown to be a matter of national concern. The title, from a statement by Sir Walter Raleigh that is used as the epigraph, refers specifically to traitors ("And then none shall be unto them so odious and disdained as the traitours . . . who have solde their countrie to a straunger"), yet it can be applied to the pilots who served England well in war but who became so disdained that they can no longer make a decent living honestly.

In *So Disdained* Shute added two new characters to the company of Stephen Morris and Philip Stenning: Peter Moran, a former pilot who manages a large estate, and Maurice Lenden, who is reduced to making aerial photographs of British military installations for the Russians. Having served together in France, they meet one stormy night in 1927 when Lenden makes a forced landing on Moran's estate. Lenden tells Moran, the narrator, of his troubled life after the war: of giving joyrides in 1919, of flying passengers and mail across the Channel in 1920, of aerial surveying in Honduras in 1921. All these projects failed, and to support his wife he took a poorly paid but steady clerical job for two years — then, like an alcoholic who "falls off the wagon," he joined a one-plane air service, lost his wife, and became an auto mechanic.

Lenden's downhill progress is sufficiently detailed for us to understand why he became sick of England and went to Russia to train pilots. In Russia, he gets to use his talents and to earn the kind of money he should have received in England. And, having lost his wife because of "England's" indifference, he easily makes the step to espionage and treason. And why not, asks the narrator, for " 'what else would you call patriotism? Just being fond of the little things you've got at home, and that you don't want to see changed. A house with a bit of garden that you can grow things in, and a dog or two, and all the little inconveniences and annoyances that you couldn't really get along without. That's your patriotism' " (154). For Shute, domesticity is a chief force for civilization; and love of country is little more than an extension of the love a man has for specific citizens of that country. In short, if England cannot provide a good living for a man of Lenden's talents and an income sufficient to keep a wife and children, then England must beware of the consequences.

Why do men like Lenden continue to fly? His estranged wife gives a sympathetic but patronizing answer: " 'Music, or the sea, or . . . or flying. A man has to have his toys, and if you try and take them away from him — you just kill him' " (128). Shute never bothers to give his own explanation of the power of flight over a man's life or imagination. Instead, through Moran, who has not flown for almost ten years, Shute shows the extent of this power by having Moran betray, in absolutely deadpan prose, the pilot's fascination with techniques and methods over life itself:

When I was taught to fly there was a rumour in the camp that it was possible to put an aeroplane voluntarily into a spin and get it out again . . . one of our own instructors, a Bachelor of Science and a schoolmaster in civil life, claimed that he had done it. So far as I remember, he had the peculiar idea that the way to get out of a spin was to force the machine into a steeper dive still; as nobody had seen him do it the first time, he was disbelieved. Whereupon he set out to show us how to do it, and it is a fact that the rotation of the machine had practically stopped before he hit the ground. I forget his name now. That made us think that there might be something in it after all. (178 - 79)

The effect here is intense and liberating: the former schoolmaster's name is not remembered because it is not important; his deed alone matters; and his deed is presented straightforwardly, almost abruptly.

Shute gains sympathy for his characters and makes his subject interesting through his own obvious love of aviation, but the best reason for reading the novel today is for its handling of the transitions and tensions brought about by aviation. At the time of this novel, England and the civilized world were going through a period of highly accelerated change brought about by the new technology. Five or ten years earlier, it would not have been possible for a spy to fly over England taking pictures at night. Maurice Lenden's dilemma is archetypal of the twentieth century: does he owe loyalty to a country or to a world-wide, world-shaking technology? " 'Maurice didn't think about being a spy,' " says his wife. " 'All he ever thought about was the job — the flying, and whether he'd be able to keep his course all right, and how he'd be able to find out what the wind was doing, and what height he'd have to be when he let off the fireworks. . . . You see, it's his profession. . . . He gets so keen upon a job, and he does his job so well for its own sake, that he forgets about the rest of it' " (148 - 49). Are we to read this passage in the hellish light created by many scientists and soldiers and bureaucrats just "doing their job," or can we take a more optimistic reading: that technology cuts across borders; that loyalty to a technical calling is higher than loyalty to a country?

In terms of plot, *So Disdained* is a reprise of *Marazan* with another threat to England and with another narrator whose patriotism is objectified through love of the English countryside; moreover, the narrator in each novel helps an outcast after a plane is forced down and finds it necessary to go to Italy. Whereas the danger in *Marazan* comes from drugs being smuggled into the country, the problem in *So Disdained* is that secrets are being smuggled out of the country. The plot centers around photographic plates of secret installations made by Lenden who, in a change of heart, goes to Italy to retrieve them from the enemy. When Moran flies to Italy after Lenden, he joins Philip Stenning (who, we learn almost parenthetically, has married the girl he met in *Marazan*) and a clutch of friendly Fascisti, "a fine, straight body of young men" (212). Lenden retrieves the plates, but he is killed in the process, thus making conventional literary restitution for his sins.

Although the American edition was thrillingly titled *The Mysterious Aviator, So Disdained* is not chiefly "about" Lenden; the character who caught Shute's imagination is his narrator, Peter

Moran. A former law student, Moran, who is fonder of the country than of chambers, has become an estate agent and is, therefore, intimately involved with the seasons, with crops, and with livestock. Still and all, Moran is a modern man — his hobby of composing music for the "silent" films not only proves his modernity but links him to Shute, who wrote to please others. Lenden and the tensions of international intrigue drop into Moran's bucolic existence — and, in a sense, into the quiet lives of the readers, since Moran is the kind of man most readers can identify with: if adventure comes to Moran, it can come to us.

What happens to Moran later happens to so many of Shute's heroes that it almost seems as if the young novelist had adopted, as his major technique, the involvement of an ordinary man in events beyond his capacity to handle. In at least half of his novels, Shute employs the same technique of lessening the central character's apparent qualifications for dealing with the unusual events that occur to him. In *What Happened to the Corbetts,* for example, an ordinary young lawyer and his family react to aerial bombing; in *Pied Piper,* an elderly lawyer shepherds a group of children through France in the early days of the German occupation; and in *Trustee from the Toolroom,* a middle-aged nonentity, untraveled and almost without economic resources, travels around the world to a small Pacific island to recover a legacy in diamonds.

IV   *End of the Airship Project*

Nevil Shute produced escapist fiction, but with a difference: none of his characters escape from responsibility; their adventures always call upon them to assume more responsibilities than they have ever had. He assumed that readers like to be told that they, by analogy with characters resembling themselves, are capable of carrying on the world's work. I think, however, that Shute's own willingness to take charge and to do more than is ordinarily expected makes the theme of responsibility so appealing to him. As evidence of the extent of his responsibility, Shute, just thirty years old, was made Deputy Chief Engineer in name but Chief Engineer in fact of the R.100 soon after the publication of *So Disdained* in the summer of 1929. Instead of starting a new novel, Shute devoted himself to the flight trials that culminated in his airship's successful flight to Canada the following summer. Nor did he begin another novel while he was in that position of responsibility.

The R.100 returned from Canada in mid-August, 1930 and never flew again — for, after the R.101 crashed in early October, the R.100 was subsequently sold for scrap. The failure of the airship venture must have struck Shute very hard, especially since he had been sufficiently concerned with the potential of long-range flying as a means of rapid communication to write a novel on the subject ("*Pilotage*"). At about the time Shute joined the airship project, Sir W. Sefton Brancker, the director of civil aviation, wrote in the foreward to Alan Cobham's *Skyways:* "I trust that the reader will bear in mind the vital importance of rapid communications to the British Empire. These journeys are but small beginnings of the vast network of regular air transport lines which will circumnavigate the globe in the future. The British must play a leading part in this great development — or cease to be an Empire."[4] The R.101 disaster ended, for many years, Britain's dream of rapid air communication with the Commonwealth countries; for two of the nation's greatest proponents of airship development, Lord Thompson and Brancker himself, had perished in the crash. Its supporters dead, the American depression under way, and the European depression deepening, the airship project was abandoned in late 1930 because of the general indifference that Shute described in his account of the R.100's return from the New World: "There were about fifty cars there to see us arrive. We slunk in, unhonoured and unsung in the English style."[5] These bitter words come from an article Shute published in May, 1933, shortly before Hitler became chancellor and before German rearmament began in earnest.

That lighter-than-air development had reached a dead end and that the heavier-than-air machine was soon to prove itself over long distances and at great speeds were beside the point; for England, in Shute's eyes, had abandoned a line of research of great potential value to national commerce and defense. "In Germany and Soviet Russia," his 1933 article declared, "in France and the United States, airship development is being pressed ahead. When we decide to take the matter up again it will be necessary for us to go abroad for guides."[6] But Shute could and did do more than merely shame his countrymen: as soon as he saw the airship project coming to an end, he began starting his own company to build planes for commercial use.

CHAPTER 3

Airspeed

I Beginning a New Career

THE crucial year for Nevil Shute was 1930: he began it in charge of a large engineering staff and ended it out of work, busy in search of venture capital for a new company, and about to marry. "It was a troublesome time for me to be out of a job, because I had got myself engaged to be married during the summer while I was somewhat tied up with other occupations of less importance. Frances Heaton was a young doctor at that time on the staff of the York Hospital, and I must say she took the loss of my job remarkably well, as she has taken all the succeeding crises in our lives" (*Slide Rule*, 144). Although marriage is an important theme in almost all of his books and although his was a successful union, Shute limits discussion of his marriage to two meager sentences in his autobiography and mentions his wife and family elsewhere only in passing. A highly developed sense of privacy and the reticence of his time and class may explain this silence concerning his family; I think, however, that after writing many novels with fairly "romantic" subplots, Shute wanted to write one story, if only his own, in which a man's work occupied the center of the stage without interruption. Besides, many men get married and have families, but how many start successful corporations in their thirty-first year?

When the airship project ended, Shute was not easily employable, as the established aviation firms already had full senior staffs. Too proud to take a lesser-paying job or less authority, and hating to see a good technical team disperse, Shute spent the winter of 1930 - 1931 traveling around England trying to sell shares in Airspeed Ltd., his new company, and to find prospective buyers for small passenger planes. Frustrated and lonely, he began to write *Lonely Road*, which is about a young man who is trying to keep English coastal shipping viable, just as Shute himself was trying to show there was still a place for the small firm in aviation. It is hard to say whether starting a corporation, a novel, and a marriage at the beginning of an international depression was foolhardy or romantic. In any case, all three prospered: the marriage lasted until Shute's death thirty years later, Airspeed grew and grew until it was absorbed by de Havillands during the war, and *Lonely Road* was his first commercially successful novel and the first of many to be filmed.

In April, 1931, Shute and Hessell Tiltman, a designer, were appointed joint managing directors of Airspeed; but Shute was chiefly concerned with administration. At about the same time, Sir Alan Cobham ordered two ten-passenger aircraft. In the early summer of 1931, Shute finished *Lonely Road;* but, swamped with administrative duties and with growing family responsibilities, he wrote no more novels for six years. His abandonment of writing novels at the time of his first real success shows the strength of his commitment to engineering and industry rather than to fiction. A cousin who worked for him at Airspeed did not even know Shute had written novels; Shute never included writers among his closest acquaintances; he seemingly preferred the engineers, executives, businessmen, professionals, military men, ranchers, and successful and efficient odds and ends of humanity whom he encountered in his busy life. This life and the people he met influenced his writing — not literature, for he read few novels and rarely admitted to reading any at all.

II   Lonely Road

After surveying Shute's career, William Buchan concluded that the early books showed "a certain stiltedness, and a tendency to waiver in their aim; they lack the fine finish, the almost unerring feeling for shape and balance in a story, which was to be the mark of Nevil Shute later on."[1] Though Buchan dated the start of the "true" Nevil Shute style and subject matter with *What Happened to the Corbetts* (1939), his first novel after he had turned to full-time writing, I would argue that *Lonely Road* (1931) is the first novel that shows his full powers. For one thing, the love story is more organic, more tightly related to the plot, than in the earlier books. For another, the story of the central characters does not end either successfully or happily. *Lonely Road* is an "uncommercial" love story in which the heroine is killed — and the novel itself is prefaced by a dry account by a family lawyer about the life of Malcolm Stevenson, the narrator, and about his death "after a comparatively short illness."

Lonely Road begins with a highly experimental first chapter that re-creates the narrator Stevenson's recollections about a drunken evening, preceding what seems to be (but is not) an auto accident, mixed up with confused personal references, with hospital reveries, and with a nightmarish flashback to Stevenson's massacre of the crew of a German submarine. But so sincere is the story — and Shute in telling it as he must — that its editors and readers sometimes believed more than the author intended. For instance, the preface conceit (that the novel is actually a slightly edited version of a foolscap manuscript found among Stevenson's papers after his death) is presented so straightforwardly and credibly that an editor at William Morrow and Company accepted it and reacted to Stevenson as a real person in her reader's precis: "I like it immensely, and I don't see how we can sell it. If Mr. Stevenson were alive I'd be more willing to gamble. But let someone else look at it. . . . I'd be ever so happy if I were wrong about its sales chances."[2] She was glad to find she was wrong; Morrow subsequently published this and twenty-one other books by Shute.

"I was evidently still obsessed with police action as a source of drama," wrote Shute twenty years later in the preface to the Uniform Edition of *Lonely Road*, "but with the growth of experience in writing, the character studies and the love story appear to have smothered the plot a bit, and these aspects of the book now seem to me to be the best." Briefly, the "police action" in *Lonely Road* deals with another threat to England that compares to the drug traffic of *Marazan* and to the Soviet espionage of *So Disdained;* the smuggling of arms into England for an apparent Communist uprising is revealed to be part of a conservative plot to discredit the Labour government at upcoming elections. A complex story, it is quite similar to the kind Graham Greene was writing in these years.

After Shute's tedious, demanding, and ultimately wasted work on the R.100, and after the tension of gambling a year of his life to put a company together, he was surely seeking liberation by inventing a character like Stevenson who can operate freely and with power, who can run a shipping line without worrying about making a profit, who can drive other men to death in a finely written sea chase, and who can step before an inquest and swear "by Almighty God that the evidence which I should give . . . should be the truth, the whole truth, and nothing but the truth; an oath which I took with every intention of committing perjury" (220).

Despite his physical and emotional excesses, Stevenson is a very believable character, largely because he is much like his creator: he is a bit distant yet basically friendly; he is sincere with a tinge of cynicism; and he is interested in how things work, in business details, in what people do for a living, and in how much they earn. And Stevenson's long thwarted desire to marry is surely a reflection of Shute's own ambition. A woman who had known him since the mid-1920s wrote me that she was "very glad when he did get engaged as he really did want to get married" and that he had written her: "I wanted you to be the first to be told because, as you know, I don't have much luck in these things."[3]

But the most profound personal effect on the novel was probably Shute's horror about the kind of political machinations that brought the R.101 to disaster just a month or two before he started writing the novel. Similarly, Stevenson is moved to "tense horror" at the "hint that all that had been sacrificed and lost was staked upon some move in party politics" (226). At the same time, the motives of the plotters are not beyond the sympathy of Shute or of Stevenson, who sees that "the root of it lay in a real patriotism and a love of England, distorted but sincere. And here I may say at once that I found no villainy about the thing. Merely an overwhelming vanity, that could not brook another view of what was beneficial for this country. . . . They served their country secretly, as criminals, and the reward that they were earning was a heavy burden to be carried to their graves. They were out to fool the country for the country's benefit, and no country takes that sort of trick too well" (228 - 29).

Professor Ormsby, the Tory intellectual who has conceived and directed the false "communist plot" that leads to a dance-hall girl's violent death, tries to justify the broad rational outlook to Stevenson: " 'You must keep a sense of proportion. . . . These deaths are lamentable. But it is this country and this Empire we are dealing with. . . . Think of it man,' he cried. 'A girl that you could pick up for a sovereign in the street! What does one girl of that description matter in a thing like this?' " Stevenson's answer seems to speak for his creator as well: " 'Leeds is a town as well as Cambridge, but about thirty times as many Englishmen live there. And you know nothing of them, nor of Birmingham, nor Newcastle, nor Manchester. You've lived your life out in this little hole among your little class, and yet you've got the most disastrous conceit to legislate for them, the people that you do not know. How do you know what may be good for them or bad, or what they may do or they may not do?' " (237 - 38). Thus, when Stevenson drives this untraveled don to suicide, his motive is an upwelling of basic human drives: he is a lonely man who is punishing Ormsby for having killed the girl he loved, but he is also a well-born democrat by choice. An incipient man of the people, he is casting down an intellectual villain by making Ormsby jump from his study's high window.

Though Shute was a Tory by birth, upbringing, and association, he was consistently liberal concerning the potentials of the individual human being; and, though his hatred of another Labour government and what he considered the foolishness of the British electorate would drive him from England less than twenty years later, he was able to end *Lonely Road* with Stevenson's confession of faith in the democratic process: "I thought that the election that was coming would be nothing but a phase in history, a milestone in the journey of a country which is capable of governing itself as competently in the future as it has done in the years gone past. . . . On the next day I went back to work."

III   *Gives up Writing*

Death alone keeps the typical Shute hero from a stoic return to his daily rounds. Henry James often wrote about tourists; Ernest Hemingway's heroes are frequently on one or another kind of holiday; but Shute's are always at work — even in *On the Beach*, they work to the last as the world is about to end. Likewise, Shute was busily at work on other things while he wrote all of his early novels; and his description of Captain Rawdon, Stephen Morris' employer, would fit Shute the executive: "There had been nothing very striking about him; he never saw reporters, never walked about London in flying kit, never did anything that got into the daily papers, never made records of any sort. He had merely gone on in a stolid, bovine manner, building rather good machines in a shed . . . and risking his life upon them daily with about as much emotion as he would have devoted to the manufacture of jam" (*Stephen Morris*, 34).

It is hard to say how much credit for the success of Airspeed should be given to Shute, but it is interesting to note that the company grew in the pattern of some of Shute's fictional enterprises. Because Shute and his associates had little capital to start, because they were ready to work, and because they had to prove themselves by getting something, *anything*, into the air, they built a high-performance sailplane that set British gliding records for altitude and distance — and with a German pilot, Shute shamingly reminds the readers of his autobiography. Certainly, Shute acted as though the enterprise depended entirely upon himself: having encouraged investment in Airspeed, and fearful of throwing his employees into the Depression's growing pool of the jobless, he felt he could give no time to writing and stopped almost completely. Although he claims to have stopped entirely, he did publish in these years several articles about aviation in *Blackwood's Magazine* — the first, an account of the R.100 airship venture; the second, a penny-dreadful novella about the decline of air circuses and the increasingly "serious" nature of aviation.[4]

His sacrifice relative to writing was worthwhile as far as the company was concerned, for Airspeed survived the Depression and grew by doing pioneering work in retractable landing gear (for which Shute and his codirector were elected Fellows of the Royal Aeronautical Society in 1934) and by helping Sir Alan Cobham develop his in-flight refueling techniques, as well as by producing successful and attractive aircraft. The Airspeed portion of *Slide Rule* reads like a modern *Autobiography of Benjamin Franklin,* for Shute takes the same pleasure as Franklin in showing how a business grows by constant attention to detail and by filling a public need: "I started an aeronautical college, a three years' course for a premium of 250 guineas which attracted a good many young men. At that time there was a marked shortage of suitable recruits for the sales and the design side of the aircraft industry . . . we turned out a number of young men in the next five years who quickly attained the highest positions in the expanded aircraft industry of the war" (202).

But, as Airspeed grew in staff and output, its indebtedness grew so much the company showed no profits during the eight years Shute was joint managing director. In fact, only England's gradual rearmament saved Airspeed from eventual bankruptcy. And once saved, Airspeed grew bigger and bigger until Shute lost all pleasure in the enterprise. In addition, rearmament meant dealing with government bureaucracy, Shute's *bête noire.* What the novelist-engineer-businessman *did* enjoy was the kind of give-and-take, free-enterprise war-mongering offered by such small clients as "Yellow Flame Distributors Ltd.," a nominal film transporting company that bought a long-range racing plane and asked that bomb racks be fitted beneath the wings for carrying film. Shute, ever moral, refused to fit bomb racks to a civilian plane; but, ever the practical businessman, he agreed to "provide certain lugs under the wings to which they could attach anything they liked" (205). This particular plane turned out to be for Haile Selassie's army; but it, like a number of other Airspeed craft, was used on one side or the other in the Spanish Civil War. Reality was beginning to resemble an early Nevil Shute espionage romance.

Official rearmament work, on the other hand, did not tempt Shute. It meant an end to designing, building, and promoting new planes; it meant building endless numbers of the same utilitarian design for the Royal Air Force; it meant extreme repetition and cost control; it meant Airspeed would no longer be an individual company building a reputation for new ideas, but part of a larger industrial machine. War work meant, in short, boredom.

IV *Resumes Writing:* Ruined City

Ironically, rearmament also meant Shute could start writing again. With the government contracts in the fall of 1936 that insured Airspeed years of work and guaranteed profits, Shute no longer felt the need to devote all his energies to his work and started *Ruined City* after a silence of five years. In addition to the easing of his worries or duties at Airspeed, the filming of *Lonely Road* in 1936 contributed to his return to writing. Shute had found visits to the Ealing Studios to watch the filming "an interest and a diversion from the frustrations of the growing aircraft business of those days." In the next paragraph of his autobiography, he tells of starting to write *Ruined City* and ends the paragraph with the same verbal formula: "It was a relief to turn to something that would take my mind off Airspeed and its troubles, for by that time I was often at variance with the other members of the Board" (231). Typically, he invented a character with even more troubles: Henry Warren, the director of a London banking house, decides to buy and reopen a deserted shipyard in order to restore the economy of a "ruined city," to keep alive British naval supremacy, and to have some "damn good fun."

The perceptive analysis of Shute by David Martin, an Australian novelist and critic, could easily be applied to Warren: "His career with Airspeed Ltd., and his sermons on venture-capital and investment, show him as a slightly disoriented pioneer in the age of monopoly."[5] Many of the motives and traits of Warren and Nevil Shute are interchangeable: both are hard-working, imaginative men who have great faith in English industry and in their mission to provide work — but they are not above cutting a few legal corners to do so. Henry Warren goes to prison for writing a falsely optimistic prospectus for his shipyard — and Shute himself, to keep Airspeed viable in 1934, had gained "a reputation with my co-directors and with my City associates for a reckless and unscrupulous optimism

that came close to dishonesty. . . . Many men drafting a prospectus
have taken a quick glance inside the prison door, and some of them
have subsequently entered it, but very few, if any, have written
about their dilemma" (*Slide Rule*, 195 - 96).

Though begun in 1936 and published in 1938, the main action of
Ruined City covers the period 1933 to 1934 — a crucial period in
European history, during which German nationalism brought Hitler
to power and prepared for World War II. Genuinely frustrated at restrictions on the British aircraft industry while Germany was rearm-
ing, Shute indulged in wish fulfillment when he had Warren win a
shipping contract away from Germany (he does so with the aid of a
Corsican dancer in a Balkan nightspot and in collaboration with a
sentimental cardsharp — romantic claptrap hopefully not based on
Shute's unsuccessful attempts to sell planes in Greece in 1935). By
the time the novel was published, English readers must have been
willing to forgive Warren any trespasses necessary to reactivate a
deserted English shipyard in time for the coming war.

All of Shute's earlier novels had contained patriotic appeals of one
kind or another: it was good business for someone who had placed
his economic chips on aviation to take a highly patriotic line. *Ruined
City*, however, differs from the earlier stories by giving Warren's
change from rational banker to practical philanthropist the force of a
religious awakening sufficient to make him a holy criminal. In many
ways, the roots of the quasi-religious *Round the Bend*, Shute's best
novel, are to be found in Warren's regeneration.

This regeneration begins when, physically and emotionally
drained by work and by the breakup of his marriage, Warren goes
into the country near the Scottish border for a walking tour. A series
of mishaps result in his being placed in the public ward of a provincial hospital for an emergency operation. Finding himself in one of
the most appealing fairy-tale situations imaginable — that of the
prince playing pauper — he hides the fact that he is a prominent
banker and stays in a ward full of out-of-work laborers. After he has
assumed their identity and begins to live like them, he quickly feels
sympathy for the town's jobless, a sympathy he could not muster in
London a few years earlier when a proposition to reopen the local
shipyards had been placed before him "not once, but many times. It
had been hawked round the City in its later stages like a vacuum
cleaner" (61). Shute efficiently motivates this growing sympathy by
having Warren watch men die in the ward after minor operations —

die because they lack hope and because their constitutions have been weakened by welfare diets.

Responding to the plight of the ruined city, Warren takes great financial risks to provide jobs; as a result, he is hounded to prison by a hypocritical and greedy clergyman who is representative of all the conventionally moral citizens who have allowed skilled English working men to be unemployed. Prison is worth it, Shute insists, if a man's stock continues to rise, if a man can come out of prison a few years later to find a young woman waiting for him, and if he finds a public memorial reading "HENRY WARREN / 1934 / HE GAVE US WORK." Cynicism aside, Shute handles the prison scene very well. If the wages of doing good are prison, then a man should be a saint in a cell. For Warren, imprisonment offers "a life of pure contemplation in conditions that were comfortable and yet sufficiently ascetic. His position was entirely comparable to that of a novice in a monastery . . . and Warren found in prison a great part of the peace that a more devout man might find within a monastery" (267 - 68).

Much in *Ruined City* strikes us as surprisingly "modern": the call for involvement, commitment; the Thoreauvian attitude toward respectability and prison. This novel quickly became Shute's first commercial success, selling twenty thousand copies within its first six months in America (where it was titled *Kindling*). Critical reception ranged from the *New Yorker's* blasê "Lord Bountiful hokum, cleverly, expertly pasted together. Will probably be a best seller"[6] and the *New Republic's* "an ingenious tale that coasts along briskly on a roadbed of utter nonsense"[7] to careful attempts to look beyond the creaking mechanism to the author's sincerity: "I think it is the author's sense of the importance of what he is writing about that submerges the details and the means."[8]

V Success

Shute's five-year respite from writing seems to have enabled him to break away from the interlocking Stephen Morris-Philip Stenning axis of his first five books; for he never returned to these characters or to the same kind of adventure plot. Nor did he find it necessary to abandon writing in favor of business: in April, 1938, he resigned from Airspeed in order to end the internal warfare between the sales and manufacturing divisions, which he headed, and the design and engineering staff. He explained the break this way: "I would divide the senior executives of the engineering world into two categories, the starters and the runners, the men with a creative instinct who can start a new venture and the men who can run it to make it show a profit" (*Slide Rule*, 237). Shute was a classic starter; his mirror image, the runner who continued with Airspeed until it was swallowed by de Havillands during the war, explained it to me another way: "Nevil had too much imagination to be a managing director." Yet, without that imagination, Airspeed, whose very name sprang from Shute's mind, might never have started or grown to a firm employing well over a thousand workers.

Ironically, the very month that Shute resigned from Airspeed, the *New York Times* noted that the novelist "Nevil Shute" had declined to reveal his true identity because "he is a prominent English business man and he says that coming out from under his pseudonym would hardly do his firm any good."[9] Although Shute had helped found Airspeed and had devoted many years of hard work to its growth, he admitted to a friend that he was pleased by the settlement he had received from the company in exchange for breaking his service agreement: it was enough to support him for five or six years while he began to learn how to make his living as a writer.[10] But, even as he was in the process of surrendering one career to begin another, his American publishers were busy giving *Ruined City* the kind of massive prepublication promotion usually reserved for a best-selling writer. In the summer of 1938, Shute took a long-deserved rest before he started his new life when he went to France for a holiday in the Jura mountains with his wife. There he received a cable announcing that the film rights for *Ruined City* had been sold for thirty-five thousand dollars, enough to double his years of economic freedom. He had suddenly become a successful, professional writer.

CHAPTER 4

Stirring Up the Hornet's Nest

I *The Shape of Things to Come:* What Happened to the Corbetts

"WHEN my writing became profitable," said Shute in an interview many years later, "I was glad to leave the office for the wider life of the novelist, though I have little respect for writers as a class. I think that a man or woman who does nothing else in the world but write novels is a poor fish."[1] He was to have little time to be merely a writer in the two years between leaving Airspeed and joining the Royal Navy in mid-1940; but he used it well, producing *What Happened to the Corbetts, An Old Captivity,* and *Landfall.* In addition, he, like the old fire horse, worked on experimental aircraft and on new weaponry in anticipation of the coming war.

When Shute returned from his vacation in France, he quickly found the topic for his first try as a professional writer, a topic very close to home: the Air Raid Precaution experts were sure that the Germans would be using lethal gases against the civilian population when the war came, and Shute's physician wife was kept busy giving anti-gas instruction at a local hospital. Shute was annoyed, to put it mildly: "My own experience of aircraft convinced me that this was nonsense. I put my fury at the misdirection of A. R. P. into a novel in which I said what I thought would happen in the event of air attacks."[2] With a firm knowledge of the possibilities of the aerial warfare he had helped create, Shute felt the anti-gas preparations were busywork that distracted the civilian population from the more likely dangers of high explosive, fire, and disease. Engineering and running a large corporation had given him "a sense of realism in practical affairs which made me impatient when less realistic minds became involved in engineering business and bred in me a cynicism for the activities of statesmen and of civil servants."[3] Shute was correct about the coming war — in reality, as in the novel, gas was not used against the civilian population.

Ordeal, the American title of *What Happened to the Corbetts*, best describes what was happening to Shute. He had changed careers in early middle-age, he had changed his English publisher (not a casual switch for a man as stable as Nevil Shute Norway), and he had even changed his usual subject matter and concerns to write his first book set in the future; his first one not dealing directly with engineering, flying, or business; his first one to treat a whole family rather than an unattached male; and the first to introduce his "little man" theme. As the novel opens, Peter Corbett, a young lawyer, is sleeping in the garage with his wife Joan and their three children, Phyllis (six), John (three), and nameless baby girl (Shute's own children, Heather and Shirley, were the same ages as Phyllis and John). The Corbetts are in the garage because their city is being bombed, but they should be either safely in a deep shelter or comfortably in bed. However, the Corbetts are surprised and confused: to Corbett, the typical middle-class Englishman, war means at first that the Englishman's castle, his home, no longer works; he finds he has no phone when he tries to telephone about the electric failure, then that he has no water, that it is raining in through his broken windows, and that (most dreadful of all) the sewer has backed up into his toilet. " 'Mine did the same,' " says a neighbor. " 'Terrible mess it made — all over the place. Unhealthy, too — not what one ought to have about in the house at all' " (34). It gets so bad Southampton begins to smell, says Mrs. Corbett, like an Italian town.

Clearly, Nevil Shute had just the kind of dry sense of humor needed by the times, and this quality explains to a large extent the popularity of such an unlikely best-seller. Actually, the humor is restricted chiefly to the first chapter and grows out of inappropriate responses to new stimuli. For instance, the morning after the first raid, Corbett goes off to his chambers clean shaven, "spruce and neat in his business suit, bowler hat, and dark overcoat, and carrying a neatly furled umbrella on his arm" (21). Never again in the novel does he dress like a respectable middle-class citizen. After Shute has enticed the shy reader into the story by making him wonder what will happen next to the Corbetts, he turns to less humorous and commonplace scenes to make his warnings.

In line with the intention Shute stated in his afterword — "If a writer has any value to the community it is that of using his imagination to foresee what lies ahead of us" — his British publishers distributed a thousand free copies on publication day in April, 1939, to Air Raid Precaution workers and officials. Most of what Shute foresaw transpired: heavy bombing, broken water and sewer lines, and epidemics. By and large, the English population responded intelligently and quickly to the blitz; world opinion was outraged by the bombing of civilians, and other countries rushed aid; the Royal Air Force recovered from its first shock and began to disrupt the bombing raids; and men evacuated their families to safety, then joined the armed forces (like Corbett, Shute was soon to send his family to Canada and join the navy). Many small details were to be echoed in reality. For instance, the Corbetts, escaping bombing and disease in their small yacht, rescue the crew of a plane downed in the English Channel in an episode prefiguring the evacuation of Dunkirk by weekend sailors. We can fault Shute's crystal ball only for seeing the Corbetts flee to France in order to get transport to Canada — Shute's aviation work had made him so sure there would be a massive air war first that he did not foresee the rapid German conquest of France before the onset of the Battle of Britain.

Although Shute had written the novel under the theatrical title of *Overture*, his British publisher rightly insisted on the understated *What Happened to the Corbetts*, which shifts the emphasis from the future to the past. War *has happened* to the Corbetts. The great advantage of choosing an ordinary family rather than a heroic pilot for the central character was a matter of strategy, for Shute wanted to reach the greatest number of people as deeply as possible by focusing on disrupted home life and endangered children. By doing so, he posed problems for his readers: if Englishmen don't prepare *now* for the war that *is* coming, *what* will happen to them and their families? One answer: they will have to steal milk for their children, as do Peter and Joan Corbett when they take fifteen cans of hoarded milk by force from a grocery store tended by a child. Shute argues through one of his typical knowledgeable figures, a surgeon, that a family man's first responsibility is to get his children to safety in Ireland or in America. This charge is practical, not sentimental, for children are a natural resource: " 'The country's going to need them presently' " (81).

Shute was more, however, than a cold-blooded rationalist arguing for preparedness. Like Winston Churchill, he knew England would need moral and emotional strengthening — a good old-fashioned uplift. Thus, the second part of his strategy is to have the novel predict that the ordinary man, the little man, will respond correctly and as decently as possible. " 'We're not famous people,' " says Mrs. Corbett, " 'and we've not done much. Nobody knows anything

about us. But we've . . . lived quietly and decently, and done our
job' " (277). The little man muddling through, like H. G. Wells' Mr.
Brittling, is a theme that Shute was to employ, sometimes *ad
nauseam* but always sincerely, throughout his five war novels. The
last words of *Landfall*, his next novel, indicate this view: "So let
them pass, small people of no great significance, caught up and
swept together like dead leaves in the great whirlwind of the war.
Wars come, and all the world is shattered by their blast. But through
it all young people meet and marry; life goes on. . . ." Today, when
reading of the death of Mrs. Littlejohn, the Corbett's neighbor, who
"bled to death, quietly and unostentatiously, as in everything that
she had done" (95), we cannot accept as easily the message of
patience before adversity. In an age of continuing war, we would
scream stop; in an age that seemed unable to prevent war, Shute
provided models of conduct.

Since war is coming, says Shute, prepare sensibly; and, when it
does come, people should find what joy they can. Having used gen-
tle humor at the start to ease readers into his story, he keeps them
from becoming disspirited with the reminder that war can be an en-
joyable break in a man's routine, as it is for Corbett who leaves his
dull legal papers behind and takes his family sailing in the fresh air;
or war can even be glorious, as in the case of one of Corbett's best
friends, a surgeon who considers himself lucky: " 'I'm working sixteen hours a day where I'm most needed, at work that I can do damn
well . . . this is my peak, and I know it. This is what I came into the
world for. Whatever I do after this will be — just spinning out my
time' " (82 - 83). A faithful servant of the king, Shute thus helped
send England to war; after the war, his chief dramatic concern was
to bring characters down from their martial heights. One story he
attempted three times in eight years before he could finish it, *Requiem for a Wren*, contains this prediction by a young woman:
" 'Until we're dead, we Service people, the world will always be in
danger of another war. We had too good a time in the last one. . . .
What we do is to put our votes in favour of re-armament and getting
tough with Russia, and hope for the best' " (213).

What Happened to the Corbetts was one of a number of books
Shute wrote without concern for possible sales but "for himself"
because he had something he felt he must say (others are *The Chequer Board*, *Round the Bend*, and *On the Beach*). Like *Ruined City*'s
Henry Warren, he was beginning to take responsibility for some of
the world's problems and to do what he could about them. Aviation

and growing popular success as a writer had given him the freedom to write; with that freedom came the responsibility to do something for the world that had given him a good life — even if doing so hurt his sales in England. But the Americans, who were not shy about being bombed, bought one hundred and sixty thousand copies from the Book-of-the-Month Club alone, *Time* gave him a lead review, the *Saturday Review* put his picture on its cover, and the publisher of *Life* pushed the book privately. Spending a month in America in the spring of 1939, Shute was quick to follow up on the success of his book, a success he had hoped for in his afterword: "If this book shows the New World something of our difficulties . . . I shall feel that I have done a job worth doing."

This first visit to the United States seems to have been partly motivated by his desire to see Cape Cod, the setting of portions of his new novel, *An Old Captivity*. Dropping his self-imposed anonymity of a business man, he began to speak publicly about the coming war on the radio and in person. André Maurois heard him deliver a speech and was sufficiently impressed to write an article about the experience. No exact text of the speech exists, but Maurois' French paraphrase, returned to English, still sounds like the real Shute. Shute starts by saying he has been in the country for several weeks and has read with interest arguments for isolationism:

I learn that a living coward is worth more than a dead hero, that America would be wrong to plunge even its little finger into the boiling cauldron of European politics and that, moreover, Germany and Italy might have a right to their living space. . . . Yes, isolationism is a splendid doctrine. My ancestors knew this already in the nineteenth century and I intend, upon returning to London, to preach this doctrine again to my compatriots.

Certainly we English should isolate ourselves from the American continent. . . . Since the totalitarian states need living room, let us give Canada to the Germans, the British Colony to Japan, the Antilles and Bermuda to the Italians. By so doing we will have resolved the European problem. Provided with excellent bases for invasion, the three totalitarian powers will be able to strive toward the methodical conquest of American raw materials and riches, a conquest much more interesting for them than that of poor little Europe. . . .

And who knows? Perhaps at last we will be able to take our turn at earning some money by selling guns and airplanes to you. And if we feel generous and tender-hearted we might even lend you a part of these earnings thereby guaranteeing ourselves an eternal and plausible cause of complaint against you.

Gentlemen, I thank your press for the precious education it has given me.[4]

All of this speech, says Maurois, was delivered calmly and surely in a
style reminiscent of Benjamin Disraeli in the time of Sir Robert Peel.
Or, I might add, Shute's style might be that of Benjamin Franklin as
he addressed the burghers of England in "Rules by Which a Great
Empire May be Reduced to a Small One" or in "An Edict of the
King of Prussia." In any case, Shute's audience, at first restless and
resentful, soon tumbled to his deadpan and smiled at the irony and
justice of his remarks.

II   An Old Captivity

Having done his bit to warn his countrymen of what was coming,
and knowing he would soon have to go to war, Shute indulged
himself by writing a story that had long appealed to him. This novel
was *An Old Captivity*, a tale with emotional roots deep in its author.
All through what he called "the heroic period of aviation," Shute
had worked at building planes and thought "it would be fun to write
a book about a difficult long distance flight. From the start, I wanted
this book to show that great flights are not made by flash-in-the-pan
heroes, but by men who can work eighteen hours a day at tiring,
menial jobs, men who are prepared to kill themselves with
overwork. . . . Those are the sort of men who made the great flights
that established civil aviation, and that was the sort of man I wanted
to write about."[5]

He had made a start on such a book in "Pilotage" fifteen years
before and in an unpublished short story probably written in the late
1920s.[6] But, since transatlantic flights became more common in the
1930s, a good part of the dramatic interest evaporated. Not until he
came across Fridtjof Nansen's *In Northern Mists*,[7] a two-volume account of Arctic explorations through the ages, did the story he
wanted to tell fall together. From Nansen, Shute learned of Haki and
Hekja, two Scottish runners who supposedly accompanied Leif
Ericksson to Vinland the Good. Shute claimed that additional
research into Icelandic and Greenland sagas convinced him that the
stories were plausible, that the two Scots were the first explorers of
America. At some point his projected story of a long-distance flight
and his interest in the early Norse explorations westward from
Greenland were mixed, and he decided to write about an air expedition in search of Norse settlements in Greenland.

He began planning *An Old Captivity* almost as soon as he finished
What Happened to the Corbetts and just after the Munich Crisis in

late 1938: "I was sick of war, and war talk. . . . I wanted to forget
about war, to write something which could make me forget that
there was such a thing as war. I thought a book like that might be of
some use, if it took other people's minds away from war as it had
taken mine. . . . The year I spent on it was a very pleasant year."[8] If
An Old Captivity is escapist fiction, the escape route was carefully
chosen: a long flight westward ending on Cape Cod with the discovery of "proof" that the first European settlers and explorers of
America were two young Scots, now "quite forgotten." " 'Not
quite,' " the young Scot pilot says in the last words of the novel to
the young Scotswoman at his side, " 'We shall remember them.' "
And the book seems to whisper that isolationist America should
remember her other strong ties to Great Britain.

Still and all, the motive for the novel that Shute gives — pleasure
and relaxation from the war tensions — is fulfilled. This is a novel of
wish fulfillment for Shute who himself would have liked to take part
in a long-distance flight in a light plane. His early lack of money,
then his responsibilities at home and at Airspeed, prevented such a
scheme. Soon after the war ended, he piloted his own plane to
Australia and back; but, in 1939, he had to content himself with a
book.

As is proper in a book written for relaxation, *An Old Captivity*
opens in a very low key on a slow train between Paris and Rome: "as
the darkness fell and the line began to climb up into the Jura Mountains the train went slower and slower, with frequent stops for no apparent reason. It was that difficult hour in a railway train, between
tea and dinner, when one is tired of reading, reluctant to turn on the
lights and face a long, dull evening. . . . It was raining . . . grey and
depressing." Their trip interrupted overnight in the mountains by a
derailment farther up the line, two ordinarily busy men — a psychiatrist traveling to Rome for a consultation; an airline pilot headed
to Brindisi to pick up a plane — settle down over their wine in a
perfect fairy-tale setting: "Darkness had fallen; there was nothing to
be seen from the windows of the train but the little station platform
on one side, and the swaying of the branches of the trees on the
other. We were marooned right in the middle of a forest, miles from
anywhere" (5). In this classical literary setup for turning inward,
Ross, the pilot, begins to ask the psychiatrist for his professional opinion about the disturbing dreams he had had five years before.
" 'We've got a long evening before us,' " says Doctor Morgan, the
psychiatrist-narrator, in the tradition of the Somerset Maugham

storyteller. " 'Would you like to tell me about it?' " (9).

The rest of the story is very simple. Through Morgan, Shute recounts the flight of Ross, Cyril Lockwood (an Oxford archaeologist), and Lockwood's daughter Alix to Greenland on an aerial photo survey in search of Norse ruins that show Celtic influence. Because Lockwood, in his layman's ignorance of the prior support and the planning needed for such an enterprise, has not prepared for it properly, Ross physically exhausts himself in preparing for the flight and then has to be the pilot, the engineer, the photographer, and the general problem-solver. Drugging himself in order to sleep, Ross begins to have extremely realistic dream-visions of the earlier explorations of Greenland in which he and Alix become confused with two Scottish slaves (in an old captivity) who had camped in the very same Greenland cove with Leif Ericksson a thousand years before.

Reviewers who liked the technical details did not care at all for the transference of identities. "There's a broad streak of romantic mysticism underneath, and this flowers forth in the last quarter of this novel in a way to put to shame even James Hilton in his *Lost Horizon*"[9] — an astute analogy in that Hilton liked Shute's novels and reviewed them frequently and favorably. But what were Shute's alternatives for resolving or releasing the tension built by Ross' obsessive attention to detail — a meaningless crash or meaningless success? Shute chose to withdraw from the world of action to that of dream and imagination, of metempsychosis; balanced against the nuts-and-bolts reality that unhinges Ross are primitive lore, superstition, and the complexity of the human mind.

When Ross recounts his detailed dream of voyaging westward from Greenland with Leif Ericksson, Lockwood is able to explain away each detail rationally. But when Ross, flying the Lockwoods to New York at the expedition's finish, impulsively lands on Cape Cod and takes the archaeologist to a runic inscription left behind by Haki, Lockwood has to admit the dreams were "true." Ross and Alix stand hand in hand beside "their" stone as the novel ends to the silent accompaniment of a great orchestra of unheard violins. Shute had always written about the workaday world; now, facing a long war, why not indulge in dreams and fairy tales?

III   *Creating the Literature of the New War:* Landfall

All through the summer of 1939, Shute worked on *An Old Captivity* during the morning; in the afternoons, he sailed the peaceful waters around the Isle of Wight in his ten-ton sloop, *Skerdmore*, whose two Atlantic crossings under another owner he spoke of proudly. But he was not occupied with just escapist fiction and with sailing; for, from late in 1938, he had spent an increasing amount of his time with Sir Dennistoun Burney in working on new weapons and in discussing the coming war. Burney, a very accomplished and practical visionary, and Shute's superior and mentor on the airship venture ten years earlier, shared very strongly his protégé's conviction that Britain had frittered away the time she should have spent arming for war with Germany. By May, 1939, Burney had found Admiralty support for a gliding torpedo project; and, as a consultant without pay, Shute joined Burney and Sydney Hansel, a young designer he had recruited from Airspeed. Working on revolutionary ideas involving rockets and airborne aircraft carriers for the defense and patrolling of the seas, the Burney team visited arsenals and testing facilities; and they finally made flight trials of their gliding torpedo from a huge commandeered yacht stocked with good food and fine wines.[10]

After Shute's mind turned to war, so did his fiction. As a result, he began "The Lame Ducks Fly," a novel about the return of a squadron of fighter planes from Singapore to England in late August, 1939, the eve of the Polish invasion. His working notes indicate that the central action was to revolve around not the main body of the flight but around a group of malfunctioning planes under the command of a young pilot named Jerry Chambers. Obviously a military version of the difficult flight of *An Old Captivity*, the new story did not hold his attention; for, after typing out twenty single-spaced pages, he headed page twenty-one with a neatly centered "2" to start his second chapter, and wrote nothing more. Instead, probably because an epic flight across Asia and the Mediterranean area was not really vital to what was happening at home during the period of the "false" war, he moved Jerry Chambers and some of the other characters directly to England and put them on duty patrolling the English Channel. By the time this new novel appeared, the Battle of Britain was just drawing to a close; as he was writing it, France was invaded and conquered, the British were driven from Dunkirk, and the English spent a summer waiting for an invasion. Thus, *Landfall*, originally titled *A Channel Story* in manuscript, was written at a time when the English Channel was Britain's only barrier against invasion and when her navy and air force were the guardians of that barrier. Moreover, through his work

with Burney that was chiefly concerned with new weapons for
Channel defense, Shute was intimate witness to the disputes
between the Royal Navy and Air Force over jurisdiction and responsibility. From all of this experience came the new novel.

Landfall opens near Portsmouth in the roadster of Jerry
Chambers. He is doing his best to verbally seduce one Mona
Stevens, a bar maid, formerly of Flexo's Corset Works; but he can
not take himself seriously. When an air-raid warden asks him to
drive on, Chambers banters:

> "The car's broken down. We're waiting here till a horse comes along to
> tow us home."
> "You don't suppose I'll swallow that one, do you?"
> "Well, the lady did. If it's good enough for her, it's good enough for you."
> (9 - 10)

In the first English novel about the new war, Shute creates the
cocky, dashing Royal Air Force pilot who can manage a boyish grin
in spite of a stiff upper lip.

Setting the first part of the story in December, 1939, that period
before the invasion of France when the English remained unsure
how real a war they had on their hands, Shute shows the boredom
and depression of the air crews that patrol the Channel. These men
doubt the value of their work; their senior officers are tired and
irritable from the tensions of waiting for the real war. In the first
chapter, when a German submarine sinks a passenger ship, the navy
accuses the air force of being lax in its patrols, and pressure is put on
the pilots by their superiors. All comes to a head when Jerry
Chambers sights a German submarine in the second chapter: "God
had been kind to him. He was to be the instrument of retribution"
(52), he thinks, and sinks the submarine. However, an English submarine is soon reported missing; and other evidence leads the navy
to accuse Chambers of having sunk it. At this point, we learn that a
rather stupid intramural war is under way: that some navy people
want to place all patrol operations over the Channel under navy control, and that the air force, with which Shute seems to sympathize
on this issue, believes the navy lacks experience with aircraft and
that the early days of a war are no time for quarrels between the
services.

Transferred in disgrace to a bomber squadron far inland, his boredom and loneliness relieved only by a propaganda leaflet raid over Germany, Chambers volunteers for a test-flying job and ends up back in Portsmouth in an experimental outfit suspiciously like the one in which Shute was working when he started the novel. When Chambers asks what this unit does, the author himself intrudes with a footnote to the effect that he learned what the work was by chance in a secret file at the air ministry — and cannot tell. In any case, it has something to do with torpedoes or bombs dropped automatically from planes in response to the magnetic or electronic configurations of the target vessel. Shute, rushing through this novel to get on with the war, and not wanting to give away any secrets, reduces the scientific details to a sinister dial on the instrument panel of Chambers' bomber, gives Chambers a specially armored seat to protect him if anything goes wrong with that sinister dial or the infernal machine behind him, and then, quite predictably, has the secret weapon explode prematurely, causing Chambers' plane to crash.

Meanwhile, back in the bar of the Royal Clarence Hotel, Mona Stevens is putting together the clues needed to clear Jerry's reputation. By listening to various navy officers gossiping at her bar, she reaches the conclusion that *two* submarines were sunk on the same day in different areas; that Jerry had sunk the German submarine that sank the missing British submarine; and that the German submarine was following the course of the British one right into Portsmouth harbor to make mischief. When Mona has the incident all figured out, she turns to another young woman, a Wren officer, who knows "very well the bitter feelings that had been raised by the affair of *Caranx* between men over-strained by war. If it were possible to show, even by inference, that *Caranx* might not have been sunk by our own action, the gain in unity would be enormous" (230). Woman's role, for Shute, is to mediate, to save men from their own professional shortsightedness and passions.

As Shute believed the dark times needed cheerful fictions, he allowed Chambers to survive — most improbably — the crash of his plane and marry Mona. Most of his eight preceding novels ended with the promise of marriage, but Jerry and Mona are the first to reach the altar in their own story. The novel's last scene in June, 1940, shows the honeymooners on their way to Canada where Jerry will train pilots. By sending them to Canada, "a less formal country," Shute can offer a kind of guarantee that there will be no social impediment to their happiness. The reason for the happiness of this war novel is found in Shute's constantly restated insistence that a writer should serve his society as best he can; therefore, writing in a time when England was learning to cope emotionally and physically with mobilization, Shute tried to show the pleasant side of being at war. In Shute's wartime, a barmaid can marry a professional officer; in war, little men with nothing to sustain them in civilian life find something to dedicate themselves to — find the chance for heroic action.

Landfall reads today like so much fluff, but it is a remarkable product for its time and its creator. A light book in dark times is not extraordinary, but one written in the spare time of a man working on new weapons, a cheerful love story by a man deeply aware of the policies that had left England largely unprepared for war — that is strange. And oddly enough, his unsophisticated story was just right for the times, as was the novel that preceded it. The reviewer in the *Times Literary Supplement,* which gave *Landfall* a "first choice" recommendation and a lead review, mused: "If you feel that the war is not something to write novels about at the present time, perhaps the most to be expected is a patriotic and sentimental concoction."[11] But George Orwell considered other factors: "The present war, owing to its peculiar character, has not yet produced a literature of its own, but Mr. Nevil Shute's *Landfall* is a beginning. . . . What makes it interesting is that it brings out the essential peculiarity of war, the mixture of heroism and meanness."[12]

CHAPTER 5

Nevil Shute, Commander Norway

I Getting into the War

WHEN the war in Europe finally reached the English Channel at Dunkirk, Shute left his experimental work with Sir Dennistoun Burney and joined the Royal Navy Volunteer Reserve. Being too old at forty-one to take up military aviation and considering the time for theory and development ended, Shute entered the navy; for he believed that, if he and others did not physically and immediately fight the Germans at sea, the war would not last long enough for England to use her sophisticated new weapons when they were finally produced. As an "elderly yachtsman," he hoped to be placed in charge of a minesweeper or some other small boat, a command that would give him time for writing. But a few days after he joined his training ship to prepare for a trawler assignment, his identity as an engineer and executive was discovered. "Still in civilian clothes and in a state of almost apoplectic indignation,"[1] he was transferred to the Admiralty, commissioned a lieutenant, and put to work within the Department of Miscellaneous Weapon Development (DMWD) that was creating new breeds of the very same fancy weapons — the rockets and torpedoes and other gadgetry — he had just abandoned.

Shute joined the navy largely because he was tired of theoretical work and administration, and he wanted to work with boats. For years he had spent his vacations sailing, had written about the joys of sailing, and had fitted a small yacht as a refuge for his family when the war came (legend has it he was fog bound in the Channel the day war was declared). Of Sir Charles Goodeve, his superior in the Admiralty, Shute made this almost autobiographical observation: "When the War came it must have been a secret joy to him; it meant that he could give his whole life to the Navy instead of just his holidays."[2] For Shute, however, the navy meant staying on dry land; and, although he did get to sea to test many of his devices, he spent most of the war in London "living in my club and going to the office every day" (*Slide Rule*, 3).

For those who might have argued that a popular writer of the status Shute had achieved by 1940 would be best employed if he were writing morale-boosting romances akin to *Landfall* or recruitment sermons like *What Happened to the Corbetts*, Shute had a ready answer: "I have no respect at all for the writer of any age or sex who thinks he can serve his country best in war time by sitting still and writing. If he is any good as a writer, he'll find time somehow to go on writing as a relaxation from his war job."[3] For over three years, Lieutenant Commander Norway headed the engineering section of the Department of Miscellaneous Weapon Development; and during each of these years Nevil Shute wrote a very creditable and best selling war novel. Though he often wrote on navy time in a corner of the large office he shared with others, his books probably did more for the war effort than the miscellaneous rockets and gadgets he developed. In fact, Sir Charles Goodeve is said to have referred to *Pied Piper*, the first of the books Shute wrote at the Admiralty, "as one of D.M.W.D.'s most successful by-products."[4]

II Pied Piper

A common legend has it that Shute had German measles in the spring of 1941 and that he wrote *Pied Piper* in sick bay out of boredom.[5] Shute said the idea first came to him in a slow train to Aberporth, a Welsh coastal village where his department conducted rocket tests. Sir Charles Goodeve remembers the development of the story in this way: "Norway and I shared an empty compartment in that very slow overnight train. I had a good sleep on one side but he did not on the other. Over breakfast he told me that he had composed the outline of the story and asked for three days leave to dictate it to his former secretary. We were a long time waiting for the arrival of our car and he told me his proposed story in considerable detail."[6] But how did a busy man, preoccupied with creating new weapons and leading a life disrupted by air raids and separation from his family, produce in a few months a novel that affected millions of readers?

A large part of the answer is found in the novel's simple story line: an elderly English solicitor named John Sidney Howard sets out to bring two English children from southern France to England just as the German invasion gets under way; after many interruptions, he eventually crosses the Channel with seven refugee children. In addition to a journey structure with an obvious beginning and end, Shute built each chapter toward a climax — a technique making for fast writing and fast reading. Moreover, the adventures of the pied piper are set within the dramatic frame of a story told by old Howard in the smoking room of a London club during an air raid.

The short final chapter ends with the club porter observing old Mr. Howard as he shambles off into the dawn: " 'He went away for a long holiday a month or two ago. . . . But I don't know as it did him a great deal of good.' " Howard's exit returns us to the very beginning when he trips over the doormat entering the club and warns the same porter to put it right or " 'One of these days you'll have me falling dead at your feet. . . . I don't want to die on a doormat.' " The narrator, witnessing this exchange, remarks that Howard seems " 'very much concerned about his latter end' " (3 - 4). The old man has given his last strength to save seven children of different nationalities — British, French, Dutch, Polish, and German — and social backgrounds in order to give the world another chance.

Shute, who had little empathy with children, may have chosen a story about children because he was separated from his own; whatever his motive, he turned *Pied Piper* into an allegory of human resources and capabilities: the old man on the verge of death saves the young and sends them to safety while the strong middle generations are busy destroying one another. The rescue of the little German girl from the violence and starvation that is ahead for Europe is used to counterpoint the novel's only serious bloody mindedness, that of the Jewish child who wants to kill Germans and has developed his own tactics: " 'One thing, you should always go for the young women — not the men. If you get the young women, then they cannot spawn, and before long there will be no more Germans' " (216 - 17). An idealist would have argued that, if war so warps the minds of children, then the artist should write against war itself; however, the ever-practical Shute would have answered that it is too late to be idealistic about war after it has come, and that one does what one can to get the children out of the way and to get on with the war.

Like many other Englishmen (literary and real) in the spring of 1940, Howard is stupid about what is coming; but, when it comes, he reacts superbly. The defeat of England's army in France and its retreat across the Channel had been a great blow to the country's pride, but, instead of becoming demoralized, the English turned the Dunkirk evacuation into an occasion for national pride and unity;

likewise, the popular and official reaction to German bombing of English cities stressed the heroism of those under fire and their defenders.

Pied Piper, written after England's initial military losses on the continent, showed, through the "Dunkirk" of one old man, how England could snatch small moral and practical victories in the face of a larger but temporary defeat. A central casting Gestapo major (Otto Preminger was to play the part when the novel was filmed) may deliver threats of torture, but the Germans are confused and perplexed by the children who are playing games in the corridor outside the interrogator's office: "It found the soft spot in the armour of their pride; they felt an insult which could not be properly defined. This was not what they had understood when their Führer had last spoken from the Sport-Palast. This victory was not as they had thought that it would be" (255).

If "Nevil Shute" was not a household name in the English-speaking world before, it became one very quickly in late 1941 with the appearance of *Pied Piper*, especially in America where the novel was being serialized in *Collier's* at the time of Pearl Harbor and was made into a very popular film in time to join the stock of mild propaganda eagerly devoured by the American public as it mobilized. Typical of the favorable critical reactions to the book was that of Edward Weeks in the *Atlantic:* "In its essentials this is the English model of a war novel — firm in its understatement, clear and sympathetic in its heroism."[7] The book's American success was not a matter of chance, for Shute carefully played to his American audience — to sell not only books but the idea that England was still waiting for America's aid. " 'Over there, they want to help us,' " Howard tells the German major. " 'If they make a home for children, refugees from Europe, they feel that they are doing something worth while' " (277). But in spite of the polite things said about America through Howard and others, we get the impression that Shute saw something a little reprehensible about a great country's playing baby-sitter while England was at war.

III   *Fighting the Secret War*

A good part of the easy charm of *Pied Piper* and the two following war novels, *Most Secret* and *Pastoral*, is that they seem to be narrated by Shute or someone who closely resembles him. *Pied Piper's* narrator is a naval officer "tired after a long day of conferences about my aspect of the war" (37) who, like Shute while he was writing the novel, lives at his club and likes interesting stories. In *Pastoral*, the narrator appears at the very end as an engineer who witnesses the final scene in the main story; and, in *Most Secret*, the narrator steps into the plot as a naval officer involved in the development of a flamethrower, one of the weapons Shute himself had worked on during the war.

Though Shute's own activities in the war could have supplied other writers with autobiographical novels, he resolutely kept himself out of his books except as an observer; and he publicly dismissed his war work: "I used to sit in an office overlooking Leicester Square in the theatre district of London and design various toys and gadgets to assist the landings that were going to take place in France."[8] The toys and gadgets, however, show the range of his interests and capabilities, a range paralleling that of his novels.

Ironically, after building planes for so many years, Shute's first job in the Admiralty was to find ways of countering low-level aircraft attacks on shipping: among other things, he developed a very efficient and widely used acoustic warning device; tried out anti-aircraft flamethrowers; developed target planes; worked on the adoption of the Oerlikon, the navy's most effective anti-aircraft gun; and, in general, found better ways of destroying aircraft. But his chief concern was with rockets. Where novelist Shute had destroyed a fictional submarine in *Landfall*, Commander Norway now invented an anti-submarine rocket with a cast-iron spearhead which sank a German U-boat on its first trial. He also experimented with unmanned rocket planes, with many kinds of anti-aircraft and ship-to-shore rockets, and with a monstrous and ultimately impractical rocket-propelled device for breaching coastal fortifications. In addition, he worked on armor, ship camouflage, and methods of converting sea water for drinking (one method was to fill lifeboat water tanks with petrol to run a small still that would produce twelve gallons of fresh water for every gallon of fuel).

Under Shute's command was a staff of about eighty people, about half of them experts and technicians of various kinds. According to Sir Charles Goodeve, Shute managed to supervise this crowd without section heads or deputies; he relied on inspiration rather than on organization. Men liked working for Shute, said another officer, because "he had a very practical approach to any problem, derived from an essentially practical training. He told his young officers what he wanted, and then left them to get on with it in their own way."[9] Many were impressed by his personal style:

when British experts wondered how German dive-bomber pilots avoided blacking out at the bottom of their dives, Shute reasoned that they *did* black out but that the planes were equipped with automatic controls for bringing them out of the dive. And, when examination of a captured plane proved him right, he "treated the matter as one of everyday occurance — the proper professional attitude of the expert."[10] Shute passed through this world deflating egos and mocking the high seriousness of men at war, but he all the while smiled benignly and played small practical jokes, such as tacking a card to a colleague's new plastic armor, proclaiming it "THE ONLY ARMOUR PLATE WHICH WILL TAKE A THUMB TACK."[11]

IV Most Secret

When the threat of a German invasion ended in 1941, Shute's family returned from its fifteen-month exile in Canada. He established it in a large country house on Hayling Island near Portsmouth, and there he came to test new inventions on his own beach. His younger daughter remembers those war years as happy ones for a child, for young navy officers were around to make toys and play games. But Shute seems to have become bored with the busywork of military engineering and administration and to have chafed for a more active and less cerebral role. The literary result was his only bitter war novel, *Most Secret,* a story of secret warfare narrated by another navy officer of Shute's rank who longs to " 'be at sea with a definite job to do' " (310).

Morale-boosting had been the purpose of his fiction, but it now became the subject. Unabashedly propagandistic, *Most Secret* deals with a series of missions to Britanny that are meant to maintain the morale of the French and to prevent them from losing faith in a British victory. *Pied Piper,* written to remind the English of their close ties to France and of the necessity for making the French understand England's determination, dealt with an escape from France — now he began to deal with brief excursions into France several years before the Normandy invasion. Starting with the assumption that a ground war against the Germans would eventually have to be fought in France, thus making the good will of the French invaluable to the Allies, Shute first imagined the kind of situation that might be most inspirational to the French in a real operation; and he then found the characters to act out his fantasy. The novel thus became a literary extension of what he was doing every day in his war work: finding the right men to create and use new weapons.

The specific method chosen for boosting French morale in *Most Secret* is the violent destruction of Germans by fire. In the manner of countless patriotic writers before him, Shute justifies violence by equating victory with righteousness and his cause with God's. Early in the novel a French priest gives Charles Simon, one of the chief characters, the idea of using fire against the enemy: " 'No other weapon purges evil from the earth and rids men from their bondage to the powers of darkness. Only the simple elementals can avail against the elemental foe — faith in the Power of God and in the cleansing power of fire' " (57). Simon later paraphrases the priest's words to describe a young chemist who has found a way to inflict horrible, incurable burns: " 'This young man . . . has been touched by the hand of God for the benefit of all mankind. All that we have done has been made possible by his great knowledge of the principles of fire. . . . If he should die, or else be given to the Germans, knowledge that has been revealed to him by God goes back to God' " (290 - 91). As this passage indicates, 1942 was no time for fine moral distinctions or subtleties.

Though there is no indication that the Admiralty considered using flamethrowers as offensive weapons against German patrol boats, Shute himself experimented early in the war with a large flamethrower mounted on the deck of an old French trawler (an obvious model for *Most Secret*'s *Genevieve*) as a deterrent against strafing planes; and Gerald Pawle writes that "the use of flame in various forms seemed to hold a special fascination for naval minds. Perhaps it was an obsession springing subconsciously from the far-away days of Drake and his fire ships. At any rate the view was widely held in naval circles that 'England will again be saved by fire.' "[12]

In spite of its Kiplingesque chauvinism, however, *Most Secret* is a triumph of craft — as Shute recognized in a letter written the day before he died: "From the strictly technical point of view, I think *Most Secret* is the best formed book I ever wrote."[13] Even the reviewer for the generally unsympathetic *New Yorker* had a cautiously favorable reaction: "probably as good a thing of its kind as you're likely to come across in some time."[14] *Pied Piper*'s earlier success was largely the result of its simple cliff-hanging organization. Shute could have used the same technique in *Most Secret;* but, with typical thoroughness and with a desire for technical perfection, he abandoned his standard straight-line narrative for a highly complex organization. One obvious reason is that the story itself is more complex than his previous tales because the novel has three major characters, several important minor figures, a first-person narrator, several love stories, a good adventure yarn, and a large war in the background. Previously, Shute had always employed one obvious central character; but he was interested in this novel in portraying realistically and organically the teamwork and organization of a complex military operation. As a result, the structure is not that of the standard adventure novel; it mirrors the mind of an administrator (Commander Martin, a thinly disguised cover for Commander Norway) who is gathering and sorting information. Told through many voices and media — participants, witnesses, intelligence reports, hearsay — *Most Secret* provides, in the manner of C. P. Snow, an insider's study of the moral, scientific, military, and human complexities of war.

This technique makes the novel seem very dry, but it is not, because it reconciles Shute the writer and Norway the "doer." "I think myself that Norway was even better as a story teller than a writer," says an old friend, who reminds us that men of action have something to tell about: "Perhaps one of my happiest memories of him is of Christmas, 1941 when he was on his own and Harry Roberts asked him to spend Christmas with us at Oakshott. Here fresh from the Admiralty he kept us spellbound with true stories of escaped prisoners."[15] Because the action of the novel proper ends in November, 1941, and because the actual writing began early in 1942, Shute seemingly built his enthusiasm for the novel by entertaining his friends.

The result was a storyteller's novel built around a series of stories within stories. The novel opens, as do most good first-person adventure yarns, at the beginning of the narrator's involvement — in this case Brigadier McNeil's visit to Commander Martin to ask his aid in coordinating purposefully sensational fire attacks on German patrol boats. Interested, Martin asks the exact question Shute always asked once he had the subject matter for a novel: " 'What sort of people are the men who want to do this thing?' " (15). That question unleashes three chapters of exposition devoted to three different characters. Having assembled a trio of chief characters, Shute then returns us to the narrative frame (Commander Martin) and the main action. Since Brigadier McNeil did not actually give Martin all of the details in chapters two, three, and four, Martin presumably has gathered them during the course of the operation and has put them together in a convenient place to show why Simon, Boden, and Rhodes hate Germans so much that they want to destroy them in disgusting ways.

The only time the novelist obviously intrudes with the poetic justice of popular fiction is in the assignment of life and death at the end: Boden disappears because he wants to die, because his spirit has been consumed by his obsession with bringing pain to the enemy; Charles Simon, whose idea it was in the first place to bring fire to the Germans, surrenders to save French hostages — not only is this romantic self-sacrifice right out of Charles Dickens' *Tale of Two Cities,* but its calm deliberateness balances the passion of Boden. Colvin and Rhodes are saved for the sake of the subplot romances that Shute's readers expected. In short, the man who has nothing to live for dies; the leader gives up his life heroically; the lovers escape — all most satisfactory except to the reader who likes realism to continue to the very end of the novel.

In Shute's earlier war novels, he had set out to relax, to entertain, and to encourage his readers while setting examples for them. *Most Secret,* he claimed, "was written to perpetuate the mood of bitterness and hate which involved England in the later stages of the war."[16] Men who were close to him at the Admiralty have told me that he was not bloody minded in his work there, that he was not interested in creating horrible weapons *per se* but efficient ones. Similarly, Shute probably chose hatred as the mood for this book rather than the optimism and courage of the earlier war novels because he thought hatred would reach more readers and with more effect. In 1939 and 1940, a celebration of England's courage was needed; in 1942, with the initial danger over and America actively in the conflict, Shute saw a need for adrenalin — and supplied it.

V *Censorship*

In spite of the obviously fictional nature of the book, Admiralty censors refused to grant permission to publish *Most Secret.* Their decision was probably based on the book's realism concerning naval procedure as much as on any similarity between the plot and actual operations involving English agents on the coast of France. Moreover, Shute's knowledge of preparations for the invasion of Europe probably supplied him with many details and incidents in the story, not the least of which was the whole matter of "official" policy concerning propaganda directed at the French populace. One sign of his growing awareness of himself as primarily a novelist — rather than as a professional engineer who wrote in his spare time — was that Shute came very close to asserting himself as a writer as a result of the censorship.

Most Secret was finished by August, 1942; by the following January, he was sufficiently frustrated by Admiralty censorship to write his British editor that he was thinking of resigning his commission in protest.[17] Gerald Pawle, a former member of the Department of Miscellaneous Weapon Development, suggested to me that Shute's contemplated resignation was inspired by "a sudden fit of annoyance — [Shute] was impetuous and rather quick tempered, particularly when he encountered bureaucratic obstruction."[18] In any case, Shute swallowed his annoyance and continued at the Admiralty until after the invasion of France; and the novel remained unpublished until the end of the war when there was no longer danger of breaching security.

At Airspeed, Nevil Shute had been running his own show, controlling over a thousand men; in the Admiralty, he was only part of a machine whose outline he could not fully see. At Airspeed, he had been the youthful director of an upstart company in a new industry; in the Admiralty, he was part of a hidebound establishment. A civilian official who worked with Shute during the war asked a mutual friend "how a man as accomplished as Norway could enjoy standing at attention and taking orders from service people of higher rank and much lower mentality. . . . He couldn't understand why Norway had wasted his talents by joining the Navy."[19] The answer, of course, was that Shute loved the navy and its traditions and that he loved the opportunity for serving the country he had tried so hard and fruitlessly to serve in the 1914 war. But he was far too independent to get along with professional navy officers, too much in the habit of going over the heads of people he knew wouldn't or couldn't help him.

Most Secret marks a double crisis for its author: not only was he tempted to resign from the navy over its censorship, but he used the novel itself to exorcise his own dissatisfactions with his war work. Commander Martin, his alter ego, continually chafes at his job: " 'Somebody has to do this Admiralty work, of course, but I'd rather be at sea with a definite job to do. Here you work all day in the office, and nothing ever seems to be achieved' " (310). When Gerald Pawle asked Shute for help after the war in compiling a history of their department, Shute's initial response was:

I have sometimes been a little bit despondent about my war service as we worked on such a lot of things that proved to be useless either because they would not work . . . or because by the time the long development was over and the thing was working satisfactorily the staff requirement had become obsolete and they were not wanted . . . or because by the time development was completed the war had moved on and that particular device was no longer required. . . . Some of the things of course were some good . . . and I suppose one should be satisfied if one in ten of those projects turned out to be really useful.[20]

VI *Propaganda and* Pastoral

With victory assured the Allies in early 1944 and with the feeling that his talents would be better used writing than developing new weapons that might never be used, Shute took on his first official writing assignment in addition to his military duties. He produced a number of articles for the Ministry of Information about preparations for the coming invasion of France, and he was called away on June 1 from flight trials for a new weapon and was sent with the invasion fleet as a correspondent. His diary of the invasion of France notes that on June 3, just before embarking, he bought an anthology of modern poetry and a copy of John Steinbeck's *Grapes of Wrath* to take along to Normandy. There was something strange in his purchase of such a novel at such a time since he rarely read novels and claimed to dislike them; if his selection of Steinbeck's book was meant as a "dramatic" or metaphorical action, that would be equally strange since not even his characters indulged in such literary gestures.

After wandering around the beaches and coastal towns for about a week, he returned to work at the Admiralty almost as though he had returned from a holiday in France; and his Ministry of Information pieces were as useless as some of the weapons he had helped develop at war's end: intended as propaganda, they were never published. Shute's only contribution as an author to the war effort during this period was *Pastoral*, the short novel he finished on his own time during the final months before D-Day. "Rather a trivial little book," he admitted in a letter to a Royal Air Force officer, "written in a hurry, but it does exemplify the point that we were discussing about the value of fiction as propaganda. . . . Taking it by and large, it's probably done as much for the RAF as any other single bit of propaganda."[21] To document *Pastoral*'s propaganda value, Shute cited a 330,000 Book-of-the-Month Club distribution in America, plus 52,000 book-store sales in America alone, all within less than a year.

Despite Shute's offhandedness and the surplus of war novels when *Pastoral* appeared in August, 1944, the novel was extremely well received by the critics. The *Times Literary Supplement* gave it a "first choice" recommendation and a lead review; Orville Prescott discussed it among other "Outstanding Novels" in the *Yale Review;* and the *Saturday Review* raved about its charm and again placed Shute's picture on its cover. The *Atlantic's* enthusiastic reviewer compared Norway to John Buchan: "For four years he has been engrossed in problems of aircraft design [sic], but when he comes down with a head cold, can't sleep, or has a Sunday off, he writes — as John Buchan wrote the Greenmantle series — for his and other's relaxation."[22] This parallel is perceptive on several levels: Shute frequently cited his admiration for Buchan; both writers were alike in purpose; and, like Buchan, who spent the last years of his life as Governor General of Canada, Shute was equally a creative artist and a man of affairs.

What brought this praise to a novel as slight in bulk, theme, and plot (a young pilot goes fishing, goes on bombing raids, falls in love, etc.) was its tonal integrity, the quiet mood established in the title and epigraph: "PASTORAL, *n. a poem which describes the scenery and life of the country.* (mus.) *a simple melody.*" Perhaps the near euphoria which permeates this novel came from a sense of massive fatalism resulting from the preparations for D-Day; perhaps Shute wrote it as an antidote to tension. Whatever the source for this mood, it also appears in the Ministry of Information sketches. For example, Shute writes in the first of a series of six articles called *Second Front* about the signs of spring in late February, 1944, and about the endless truck convoys and other evidence of the invasion that will come with warm weather. This powerful little sketch ends with a naval officer saying to Shute, "Quite a feeling of spring in the air today," and Shute's reply:

I thought of the [assault craft], of the tanks, of the American convoy, of the fighters at the aerodromes, of the widening lanes, of the Hardmaster, of the Wrens chihiking with the ratings. I stood in the pale sunlight on the cold steel deck looking out over the mud flats, all pastel green and purple in the slanting light of winter. Behind me there was the purring of a motor, and the scrape of shovels shifting stones and sand from the concrete of the Hard, to clear a passage for an army.

"Aye," I said, "it'll soon be spring."[23]

The irony of waging war in the spring appealed to Shute. By setting *Pastoral* in the countryside where life was little changed by the war, he exploits beautifully the ironies of the first kind of warfare that enables a man to live in the midst of peace while he is only hours or minutes away from violent death. Though slight and on the verge of being pure escapist fiction, *Pastoral* stands out as a novel that realizes the dramatic potential of some forms of "modern" war that give man a life both normal and strange. To wage modern war, a country needs bombers and pilots; pilots need youth and health; bombers need air fields; air fields need the amount of space found only in a rural setting; a healthy young man in the country needs a girl. " 'The great adventure on this station isn't bombing Germany,' " an officer complains. " 'Falling in love is the big business here' " (149).

Given the quiet landscape that Shute's protagonist, Peter Marshall, comes home to after bombing German and Italian cities, the pastoral-amid-war conceit is perfectly realistic. Furthermore, the stresses placed upon Marshall and the other pilots demand that they attain peace of mind in order to have the nervous reserve to carry them through sudden emergencies; the long hours of monotonous flying back and forth between home and target provide the occasion for contemplation; and, as a night-flying bomber pilot, Marshall "had seen so much moon in the last fifteen months that he had absorbed a little of its serenity" (39).

Thus, when Peter Marshall wakes up one sunny spring morning to the mixed noise of aircraft and cows, he thinks first of fishing. And when, on the way to the stream, he stops to inspect the damage done to his plane the night before over Turin, his talk is chiefly about fishing. When Hemingway, in "Big Two-Hearted River," had Nick Adams go fishing to forget the war, he made the fishing almost mystical. Shute would probably have found both Hemingway and Nick puzzling, but Nick would not have approved of Marshall's lure, "a peculiar whirligig designed to represent a lame mouse taking swimming exercise, alleged to be very attractive to a pike" (12). The lame mouse works; Marshall catches a huge pike and begins a romance by offering to share it with a young woman. An unlikely cupid ("Death had not improved it; it leered at them with sordid cruelty" [20]), the pike leads to a troubled courtship and to a happy ending in spite of another pilot's refrain, " 'I always said no good would come of that fish.' "

"One would not ordinarily expect to get a good novel about this war — not yet; it has often enough seemed a waste of effort to try to get the war, as so many will try, into moderately light fiction. But if

novelists feel that they cannot leave the war alone, it could be
wished that more of them wrote with feeling as unexaggerated and
humor as warm and lively as Mr. Shute's." So wrote the *Times
Literary Supplement* reviewer[24] who recognized that the novel was
an entertainment — which Shute himself admitted. In short,
Pastoral was as affirmative and as immediate as the rest of Nevil
Shute's war fiction. Never once did he question the justice or
morality of the war itself or the actions necessary for victory. Though
the modern war novel is typically anti-war, anti-military, and anti-
officer, Shute's are atypical on all three points. The probable reason
for the difference is that most bitter war novels are written well after
the war is over and that Shute wrote his during the war while
emotions were still hot and while both writer and reader could feel
enthusiasm for the conflict. Like the weapons he invented, his war
novels served their purpose and their time.

CHAPTER 6

Peace and Expanding Awareness

I Vinland the Good

JUDGED in the light of the preceding years, 1944 and 1945 seem unproductive for Nevil Shute. They began well with the completion of *Pastoral*, but that is an almost ominous book since, though the love story works out, the characters are tired. Peter Marshall has flown too long; his request for a transfer from bomber duty at the novel's end is a "farewell to arms." A similar *ennui* appears in *Most Secret;* and, although most of the characters in both novels are vital, a suspicious number are badly in need of rest or a change. That Shute's excitement of the early war years has disappeared is not surprising when we remember that Shute had started writing about the war before it actually began and that he was well into middle age when it ended. By late 1944, he was sufficiently tired of the war and his work in it to have himself released from the navy.

Through the winter and spring of 1944 - 1945, Shute, while awaiting assignment to Burma as a Ministry of Information correspondent, tried his hand at two filmscripts. Neither was ever filmed; but *Vinland the Good*, an adaptation of the Viking episodes of *An Old Captivity*, was published in late 1946. Surely his least successful published fiction, *Vinland the Good* is his only book not in print today. The novel was his form, and he was never on easy ground elsewhere. At the same time, however, *Vinland the Good* shows that Shute was searching for new themes and subject matter. The very fact that the basic story grows from an earlier work gives us the measure of the new interests that would occupy him in most of the novels he wrote in the remainder of the decade and well into the 1950s: the role of the "little man" in history and society, the joys of finding a new life in a new land, and the problems of the returned serviceman.

In *Vinland the Good*, Shute puts an end to the war by returning to the story he wrote in 1939 as an escape from the coming war and by telling his story through a young officer who has just returned to civilian life. Shute had begun thinking about what would happen to people at war's end in *Pastoral* in which his central character, a former insurance clerk, is so indifferent to the thought of going back to the office that he does not mind the idea of being killed. For *Vinland the Good*, Shute invents young Major Callender who reclaims his prewar teaching job; but, since he has learned to think for himself during the war, he lasts only a day as a history master when he tries to make the Dark Ages "relevant."

Major Callender is fired chiefly for expressing the "little man" theme that Shute began to develop in characters like Mr. Littlejohn in *What Happened to the Corbetts*. Callender generalizes most grossly (in his author's service) that "People in history were not a different race from you and me. Your history books deal mostly with the great people, the Kings and Princes and the Ministers of State. They're just the froth upon the surface; the Kings and Princes and the Ministers — they don't mean much. History is made by plain and simple people like ourselves, doing the best we can with each job as it comes along" (125). This prose has a Churchillian beat; it is a democratic rhetoric suitable to inspirational wartime speeches. Shute not only was to bring this rhetoric into peacetime but was to put the little man at the center of some of his most successful books — *The Chequer Board, No Highway, A Town Like Alice, Round the Bend,* and others — culminating with the fullest treatment of the theme in the last novel he finished, *Trustee from the Toolroom* (1960). Oddly enough, as a perfectionist and as a bit of a snob, Shute had little patience with human failings and less love for the logical political and social ramifications of the philosophy of the worth of the common man. Thus, while the return to power of the Labour government in 1950 helped drive him from England for good, it did not drive away his idealized conception of the ordinary man.

Finally, it is worth noting again that *Vinland the Good* was written while Shute awaited transportation to the war in the East where he was to report on the fighting in Burma for the Ministry of Information. Since Shute had never traveled outside of Europe and North America and since he had requested this assignment to a part of the world he had never seen, it is tempting to speculate that the voyage of discovery in *Vinland the Good* is a metaphor for the journey its author was about to undertake. Most of the novels he was to write over the next fifteen years were to deal with similar voyages or flights of discovery, generally within the Commonwealth. So *Vinland the Good,* in that it expands a part of the novel he wrote after his first travels as a writer and before he joined the navy, signals a return, conscious or unconscious, to the author's expanding awareness and interests.

II   The Chequer Board

In Burma, Shute examined the last stages of the war against Japan and the tangled relationship between the British and the Burmese Nationalists. None of the six articles he wrote while in Burma in the spring of 1945 reflected what officials back in London wanted, and none were published. His correspondence with the Ministry of Information shows that the novelist was unwilling to turn this phase of the war into usable fictions for the home country's propaganda mills. For Nevil Shute and Commander Norway, the war was over; he returned to England in the summer of 1945 and resumed his long-interrupted career as a full-time writer.

Shute had entered the Royal Navy in 1940 as a former engineer with a comfortable income; he returned to peace having doubled the total of his published books and having established himself, without the intention of doing so, as one of England's best-selling novelists — and with an annual literary income of roughly ten to twelve thousand pounds sterling in a time when one could live very comfortably on only a fraction of that amount.[1] The war was a turning point for Shute: he came away with a far wider knowledge of the world and of the capabilities of its inhabitants — a knowledge used in his first novel of the new peace, *The Chequer Board.*

The specific knowledge that went into the new novel came from two directions — his own observations of the impact of American troops on small English towns during the war and of the influence a strange culture had exerted on him in Burma.[2] Outside of his enforced residence in London during the war, Shute had spent his adult life in Hampshire and Yorkshire among his own class; motoring up and down the Irrawaddy Delta hunting Japanese vessels in a gunboat officered and manned chiefly by brown men introduced Shute to a whole world of nonwhites efficient at their jobs. The engineer's respect for competence soon turned into a more basically human respect resulting first in *The Chequer Board* and soon thereafter in the far more spectacular *Round the Bend,* a vision of many colors and cultures linked by a commonly shared technology.

Soon after returning from Burma, Shute read a new book by

Walter White, Secretary of the National Association for the Advancement of Colored People, that dealt with the treatment of Negro troops in England and Europe during the war.[3] Interested in the case of a black soldier unjustly sentenced to life imprisonment by a military court for a rape that did not occur, and doubly interested because the incident had taken place in a small town near his home and had created great sympathy in the area for the harsh treatment of the soldier, Shute began a correspondence with Walter White. Out of this incident came *The Chequer Board*, which Shute wrote in a burst of energy between September, 1945, and February, 1946.

Starting with *What Happened to the Corbetts*, Shute's great popular success had been based upon his talent for being topical. Of course, having a major war at hand did give him an obvious subject matter of burning current interest. *The Chequer Board* gained an easy topicality by cutting back and forth between the war and the postwar years, but Shute's real talent is to be found in the way he extended the war against a national enemy into a war of more universal concern — one against intolerance. The real secret of his talent was not that he was merely topical but that he had the ability to hit upon topics that would soon be popular, even commonplace.

In other hands, the subject matter of *The Chequer Board* might have produced a far greater novel. Reviewers generally liked it, but the complaint that it was a lightweight treatment of heavy themes kept creeping in. But there, of course, is Shute's strategy: heavy books about heavy themes rarely reach the common reader — the man who must be reached if any broad change is to come about. So Shute wrote to, for, and about the ordinary man as he is represented by John Turner, who was described by an American reviewer as "a typical lower middle-class Englishman fully equipped with the prejudices of his kind, covered with the social and political barnacles which have been gathering on Anglo-Saxon consciousness since Elizabeth put the island on a paying basis, and solid with the virtues which have made Great Britain a dependable block in the arch of democracy."[4] Jackie Turner is Shute's first full-length portrait of the "little man" that he came to use *not* as his own alter ego (as were Stephen Morris, the narrator of *Most Secret*, and others) or as the adventurous figure he could not be (as was Philip Stenning) but as the alter ego of the common reader he wanted to reach.

Like Everyman, his medieval counterpart, Turner has been summoned by death. The novel begins when he learns he is about to die because his head has "gone bad." Little bits of wartime shrapnel are festering in his brain and cannot be removed; the past has caught up with him. Turner's realization that his old wound will only get worse does not raise a shout or a cry, but the quiet assessment, " 'After that, I'll die.' " " 'We've all got to do that, Mr. Turner,' " replies the surgeon-narrator in the last words of the first chapter. Although "All be the same in a hundred years" is Turner's typical reaction to any problem, his stoicism does not prevent him from trying to do something of value with his remaining time.

"All be the same in a hundred years," an expression Shute was to apply to himself shortly before his death, is not as much a creed as a futility to be overcome: all will be the same unless we do something *now*. Like the characters of Shute's most famous novel, Jackie Turner is on the beach — but what does one man do when faced with death? He gets on with his life, says Shute. Knowledge of forthcoming death frees one from the rut of life, especially if the warning comes in time. Life has passed Turner by because "there was always something more important to be done, the sheer, insistent business of living that stood before the things he would have liked to do" (26 - 27). Shute had originally called his protagonist "Worth," suggesting perhaps his essential worthiness; but the choice of "Turner" shapes his allegorical role — as one forced to turn, to change.

Although *The Chequer Board* starts and ends as Turner's story, it soon becomes the story of three other men who once shared a hospital ward with him in Cornwall. In the long third chapter, Turner sits in his suburban garden in 1948 (though the novel was published in early 1947, Shute had postdated the action) and tells his wife about these three men and their lives until 1943. Turner had been badly wounded in a plane crash; under heavy sedation to keep him from moving, his eyes bandaged, almost incapable of speech, and strapped like a mummy in a womblike environment, Turner could only listen while the other three related their life stories for him. To this archetypal storytelling situation — the bestilled voyager who must listen — Shute added the spice of crisis: Turner is caught between death from his wounds and imprisonment for black-marketeering should he survive. The other men, all very young, were also going through personal crises: the American Negro had cut his throat after being pursued by military police for what they mistakenly assumed was an attempted rape; the English soldier awaited trial for killing a man in a drunken fight; and the pilot, guilty of no crime but resentful of being in a ward full of "criminals," was chiefly concerned about his weak marriage. Turner, sitting in his garden five years later, feels somehow bound to these troubled men; he decides to see if there is anything he can do to help them before he dies.

Starting with the assumption that Phillip Morgan, the young pilot, will be the easiest to trace, Turner discovers that he is now married to a "native" girl in Burma. Oddly enough, a number of the people interviewed for this study recalled *The Chequer Board* as "That book about the Englishman who went native"; and Morgan's family in England has exactly that impression of his life. When Turner flies to Burma to see for himself, he finds that Morgan has married the educated daughter of a prominent Burmese family and that he lives a good and responsible life as an official in the new "native" government. The mistake of the interviewed Americans and Englishmen who admired Shute is enlightening; for, since their social education tells them that normal Europeans do not marry "native" women, the specific details about such a union are soon forgotten and only one "fact" remains: a white man has gone native.

Sitting on Morgan's veranda overlooking the Irrawaddy, and with Morgan's attractive brown wife listening — a scene echoing the earlier reminiscences in his own garden — Turner learns from Morgan that the charges against Dave Lesurier, the Negro soldier who had cut his throat, had been dropped. Back in England, Turner discovers that Duggie Brent, the soldier who had killed a man in a fight, had been acquitted of his "crime"; but Turner is unable to find Brent. When he then goes to the little town in Cornwall where Dave Lesurier had his trouble, he finds that Lesurier has settled there and has married the local girl he was once accused of assaulting. Like Morgan far away in Burma, Lesurier and his wife have a little brown baby. Moreover, Lesurier is able to assure Turner that all is well with Brent. His quest fulfilled, the novel ends with Turner's visiting the brain surgeon who eventually tells us the story. " 'Well, Mr Turner,' " asks this worthy in the novel's closing words, " 'what have you been doing since I saw you last?' "

The *Times Literary Supplement* reviewer saw this novel as disjointed, just as any reader of this summary might. Certainly Shute's method of telling it is complex because the four lives are fragmented and intertwined. But the complexity and the interrelatedness of life are the novel's true subjects, as the epigraph of this novel from Edward Fitzgerald's *Rubaiyat* should make clear:

'Tis all a Chequer board of Nights and Days
Where Destiny with Men for Pieces plays:

> Hither and thither moves, and mates, and slays,
> And one by one back in the Closet lays.

Although Shute usually told his stories in a perfectly linear fashion, he could depart from the straight ordering of events if another method might be more successful. Thus the complex *Most Secret* was organized in a manner appropriate to its teller, a gatherer of intelligence, an administrator. In *The Chequer Board,* to give a sense of checkeredness and to involve his readers with the characters, Shute recognized that the narrative required the fracturing of experience. For example, the narrator in London tells us about Turner's hearing in Burma from Morgan a story he (Morgan) had heard in Exeter from an American who had heard about events in Cornwall. Shute, poking holes in the convention of the narrator who knows all, reminds us that the truth is not in one convenient place but has to come from far and wide, just as the possibilities of human experience are not to be defined or limited by one race or nationality or social class.

Although the novel seems disjointed, it holds together through a web of corresponding situations, through differences that turn out to be similarities. All things are relative: Dave Lesurier finds England a paradise after racial prejudice in America, but Phillip Morgan cannot bring his Burmese wife back to England because he knows that after Burma, where she is in the majority, England would be full of bigotry. Lesurier, better educated and far more traveled and experienced than most men in the little Cornwall town he settles in, brings new blood and vitality to his adopted country, as does Morgan in Burma. Shute happily mixes his characters into a global stew, simmering them until they can no longer find their separate identities again.

The Chequer Board occasionally becomes almost saccharine, which may be why Shute has Turner divert truckloads of army sugar to the black market during the war and continue after the war in "sly illegal deals in pastry flour" (29). There is something sinister, however, in the sweetness in *The Chequer Board* because its vision of love and brotherhood comes to a man who is on the verge of death, a man who has splinters of steel festering in his head. And Shute adds the same sweetness a few years later to *Round the Bend,* in which an almost cosmic love is found in another burnt out case, a man dying of leukemia. Moreover, Shute's *In the Wet* (1953) projects yet another vision of brotherhood in the form of a malarial dream beside the deathbed of an alcohol-and-opium-besotted outcast who is dying of a ruptured appendix. Rarely was Shute able or willing to present a vision of goodness without somehow making reservations.

Beneath the confection in *The Chequer Board* is a steady unmasking of social attitudes that go far beyond racism since the obvious and glaring stupidity of color prejudice is just the window dressing. Shute presents these broader social ills through the one story that has no racial point: that of the young commando Brent who killed a man in a brawl. With Brent's case, Shute demonstrates his great interest in what justice means and in how circumstances determine our view of a matter. Using a style most genial and agreeable, Shute leads us through Brent's "elementary" curriculum as a soldier: Bren guns, Sten guns, Tommy guns, and grenades. He then presents the college course: mines, booby traps, and the realization that "you could kill a lot of people with a couple of hundred gallons of blazing oil if you went about the matter with discretion and intelligence" (46). But the real peak of Brent's education comes when he learns how to "attack an armed man three stones heavier than himself and kill him with his hands and feet alone in perfect silence. In 1943 he did so, in the dark outside a public house just off the New Cross Road" (47). What jars here is the inappropriate time and place of the killing; had Brent done the same thing in battle, no one, not even the enemy, would have thought poorly of him. But Brent kills a civilian because "he had never learned to box like a gentleman; there had been no time to teach him that" (50). Shute finds Brent not personally guilty because he had never been taught how to control the knowledge forced upon him.

Fortunately for Brent, Shute's world is one where poetic justice thrived. Thus, the young soldier is defended by a lawyer who has spent his war years teaching hand-to-hand combat. A descendant of Herman Melville's Captain Vere, he also harps upon duty: " 'it is right that you should know I serve the King in two capacities. I assist in the discovery of the King's justice in these courts . . . [and] I teach men such as Douglas Theodore Brent to kill other men with knives. I cannot dissociate my two responsibilities to the Monarch' " (314). If Brent is guilty, his defender (who wears exactly the same uniform) and the King's army are also guilty.

But Shute's imagination was not fully engaged by Brent, who is never allowed to join Morgan and Lesurier at stage center. And, though the story of Lesurier is highly important, Lesurier himself appears only briefly later in the novel. Shute, coming right down to it, is more comfortable with the kind of man he had been writing about for so many years: Morgan, the young pilot, a social and cultural *tabula rasa* — clean in 1943 except for his unquestioningly held bourgeois notions, "a callow and ignorant young man" redeemed only by an ability to "fly an aeroplane very well indeed" (56). Thus, getting locked up in a guarded ward with a black-marketeer, a killer, and an accused rapist is "an educational experience . . . very good for him" (55).

Morgan does not change dramatically in the hospital, but his fondest prejudices get such rough handling that he is ready later for a Burmese guerilla's indictment: " 'You English people think of us as naked savages. But our religion and our culture are much older than yours. In your country you have only taught the common people to read and write in very recent times. In Burma, for over a thousand years every boy has learned to read and write in our religious schools. And yet you have the impudence to think yourselves superior to us.' " British superiority amounts to only one thing, says the Burman, " 'You learned the use of firearms before we did, and conquered our country' " (158 - 59).

Morgan falls in love with his cultural tutor's sister, marries her, and stays in Burma to do good where he is needed. The politically sensitized reader might object loudly at this point that Morgan's desire to help his brown brothers is just another mask of colonial paternalism. To the liberal who says, "Get out of Burma and let the people learn to do without European help," Shute would reply, "We haven't prepared them for freedom, so let's help out." Though echoes of colonialism and mechanical superiority reverberate throughout the novel, we must not ignore Shute's own sincerity in feeling both a British and a human responsibility for the welfare of Burma as an independent state. Morgan may occasionally slip into the great white father's robes, but he does his best to disappear into the society around him. To fault him for acquiring a fine house is to suggest that "natives" do not live in comfortable abodes.

Just as Shute slips unconsciously into paternalistic attitudes in the Burmese sections, he seems to fall equally innocently into thought patterns that some would call racist. Dave Lesurier (whose French name means "the smiler") cuts his throat with that old cliché, a razor-sharp knife; Shute's model of a just man, an officer from Maine assigned to investigate the charges against Lesurier, feels disqualified because he knows "very little about Negroes," having only defended one other, "a colored janitor on a charge of stealing coal"

(268 - 69). Shute's heart is in the right place, but his little insen-
sitivities show how difficult it is even for a just man to clean his mind
of the fruit of prejudice.

In spite of Shute's small racial blunders, blunders more obvious to
today's naked sensibilities, his obvious good will is strong enough to
make the story work. He believed in *The Chequer Board*, calling it
"a sincere book which I genuinely thought would ruin my American
sales."[5] The novel turned out to be very popular in America, a fact
that helped him toward the formulation of a thesis he stated in a
letter he wrote the day before he died: "sincerity is the first attribute
for making money in the business of writing novels."[6] And on his
trip through Asia in 1948, he gave a copy of *The Chequer Board* to a
young British officer who seemed shy about marrying his Siamese
girl friend. When he learned on his way back to England that the
couple had married, he noted in his diary that "In these circumstances *The Chequer Board* went down very well." That he
would give the book to someone as a guide or an inspiration should
document his belief in the practicality and utility of his writing.
Others may accuse Shute of sermonizing, but I would counter that
the sermon, from Samuel Richardson's *Pamela* to Hemingway's *For
Whom the Bell Tolls*, is a major mode of middle-class fiction.

III   No Highway

In early 1947 as *The Chequer Board*'s sales mounted, Shute wrote
Walter White that "there is, as you have pointed out, bound to be
adverse criticism from the die-hards, and in view of the unexpected
scale of the distribution there may be quite a lot of it. In view of this,
I have decided to come over to your country at the beginning of May
to stand up to be shot at, which should be great fun."[7] Shute and his
wife spent May and June, 1947, traveling by car in the United States
from the East Coast to the South to the Midwest and back in
deliberate search of the American "man in the street." Avoiding the
conventional literary and lecture circuits open to highly popular
writers, they stayed in motels and ate in Greyhound bus stations and
small cafes. Shute fished in the Smokies, saw the Indianapolis 500,
and lectured on India at Fisk University. This crash course on
America affected him so favorably that on his return to England he
wrote a letter to the *New Statesman and Nation* that contrasted
America's good will toward Britain with the "bad temper" of British
politicians and journalists toward America.[8]

The growing dissatisfaction with his own country's political and emotional climate that made the usually reticent Nevil Shute write that letter was soon to cause him to desert England. For the time being, he returned to his old love, civil aviation, in *No Highway,* a novel that sniped at England's ever growing and ever self-serving bureaucracy but celebrated the individuality and eccentricity at the heart of England's vitality. *No Highway* took its title and epigraph from John Masefield's "Wanderer":

> Therefore, go forth, companion: when you find
> No highway more, no track, all being blind
> The way to go shall glimmer in the mind.

These lines remind us that all but one or two of Shute's novels deal with characters who travel, frequently around the world, in search of something: wealth, success, happiness, the truth, understanding, love. Travel is Shute's controlling metaphor, his passion, as the epigraph to his autobiography suggests: "To travel hopefully is a better thing than to arrive, and the true success is to labour." But it should also be noted that Masefield's lines point to a turning away from the physical world to the mind or spirit — a necessary direction, as we will see, when no other highway exists.

Superficially, *No Highway* is the story of one Theodore Honey, a frog-faced, middle-aged research scientist in the Structural Department of the Royal Aircraft Establishment at Farnborough. Ill shorn and tattered of trouser, Mr. Honey is derived in part from the eccentric scientists and specialists who supplied ideas to the Department of Miscellaneous Weapon Development during the war. Men barely capable of daily existence, they often knew one thing very well — and did well if given a decent chance. Dennis Scott, Honey's youthful superior at the Royal Aircraft Establishment, finds in Honey's neglected research files "sad evidence that we had not made use of genius that lay under our hand, in the last war" (157). Narrated by Scott, the novel becomes the story of that newly appointed young administrator's education in the complexities of the scientific mind. Although Scott's first impression of Honey is negative, he soon becomes Honey's chief apologist and supporter by going through a variation of the sensitizing process we found in *The Chequer Board;* just as Jackie Turner and Phillip Morgan and others learn to look beyond race, Scott must come to look not only beyond social form, dress, speech, physiognomy, but especially beyond a reliance upon orthodoxy in belief and in method.

When Mr. Honey, on the basis of pure research, predicts structural failure of the tailplane of a new transatlantic airliner at 1440
hours of flying time, authorities refuse to believe him largely
because he is "odd." Honey's problem is the width and breadth of
his vision; working in a world of engineers and bureaucrats who are
staring down separate tunnels, Honey claims the right to look at all
of reality and at much that seems unreal (as when he announces he
has located the missing tailplane of a crashed airliner with the help
of a Ouija Board planchette). To an official who rejects his method as
" 'too unscientific for us to put forward as evidence,' " Honey
replies: " 'It's not unscientific at all. . . . It's the product of a
carefully controlled piece of research extending over a good number
of years. The fact that aeronautical people don't know much about
research in that field doesn't prove that it's unscientific. They don't
know much about cancer research either' " (301). Not only is Honey
guilty of psychic research, but he had most unwisely published in the
1930s a paper "advocating the construction of a rocket projectile for
an exploratory journey to the moon" (144 - 45). " 'The fact that his
interests spread very wide doesn't mean he's mad,' " insists Dennis
Scott to a world racing toward specialization. " 'It means that he's
sane' " (161).

Though Honey is sane, his sanity is locked within his small, ugly
body. Flying to Canada to investigate the mysterious crash of a
Reindeer airliner after 1393 hours of flying time — close to his
prediction of structural failure at 1440 hours — he learns that he is
aboard another Reindeer that has also flown to the point of failure.
Because he looks ineffectual, weak, and nervous, he cannot convince
the crew to remain on the ground at Gander, their refueling stop.
" 'If he'd been an athletic type six feet two in height and weighing
fourteen stone, with a red face and a fist like a ham, they'd have
believed him all right' " (179), Scott wearily complains. In Mr.
Honey we again see the chequer board of existence — another
human is not working at his full potential because the world judges
him on the surface.

And the world's reaction has helped alienate Honey in a way
dangerous to the world, for the scientist must keep in touch with the
human implications of his work if he is not to create Frankenstein
monsters. Honey is so alienated when we first meet him that he
reacts with pleasure to the news of the Reindeer's crash at 1393 hours
in Canada: " 'Well, that's a real bit of luck . . . it will shorten down
our work enormously' " (37). Initially, Honey's only interest is in his

theory, not in the people who might die. Thus, he objects to acting on his theory until it is satisfactorily proven. But actually flying in a possibly doomed Reindeer with real humans burns away his scientific objectivity to the extent that, rather than let the airliner fly on from Gander, he activates the undercarriage retraction gear while the plane is on the airstrip, thereby causing seventy-two tons of machinery to crumple to the ground (the method Mr. Honey chooses was probably inspired by the wreck of the airliner that brought Shute to the United States the year before: landing in Boston, it tipped over on one side when the right-hand undercarriage retracted prematurely). Honey's sabotage is a dramatic sign that human concerns have intruded upon his ivory tower, for Mr. Honey of the first chapter would not have interfered.

In a theoretical paper over twenty years before he wrote *No Highway*, Norway the engineer predicted that a period of fifty years "would be moderate" for the development of a large, fast, safe, and economical passenger air service.[9] By the time he started *No Highway*, that passenger service had arrived thirty years ahead of schedule, showing him through his own experience that aviation could and would develop much faster than the industry's own experts could predict or prepare for. Shute wrote *No Highway* partly because he was aware of early research about the fatigue of the alloys used in modern aircraft. At the time he wrote the novel, metal fatigue (an old concern to railway engineers and bridge builders) had not yet become a practical problem in the civil aviation industry because the conditions of size and speed that would produce the alternating stresses resulting in a sudden crystalization and breaking of metal did not yet *seem* to exist. Shute had sufficient imagination and practical awareness of technical, economic, and human forces to know that, if metal fatigue *could* in theory develop, it *would*. Thus he tells us in the "Author's Note" that he returned to civil aviation as a fictional theme because "I think it important that fiction and drama, the most potent educational influences in the world, should deal properly and candidly with all aspects of modern life; this includes aviation" (345).

Just as *The Chequer Board* grew out of a combination of his own experiences and the observations of experts, so too did *No Highway*. His 1947 plane crash, his work on the R.100 and in manufacturing, and his knowledge of the economic demands of civil aviation, all contributed. But the chief inspiration for *No Highway* came from a man very much like the author himself: Sir Alfred Pugsley, a few years younger than Shute, had been one of the engineers on the ill-fated R.101, and he had been in contact with Shute from 1926 onward. As the head of the Structural Department at Farnborough (the same department headed by *No Highway*'s narrator) from 1941 to 1945, Pugsley had done original work on metal fatigue in military aircraft. Out of Shute's visit to Pugsley late in the war came the technical center for the novel and a professional role in which to insert a fictional narrator.

In March, 1949, about six months after *No Highway* was published, P. B. Walker, Sir Alfred Pugsley's successor at the Royal Aircraft Establishment and thus Dennis Scott's real-life counterpart, delivered a paper entitled "Fatigue of Aircraft Structures" before the Royal Aeronautical Society. Where Shute had imaginatively depicted the results of fatigue, Walker very cautiously opened with the words "At the present time there are indications that structural fatigue may become a major factor in design."[10] If my present book were a novel and if I told the reader that a novel about aircraft fatigue failure appeared in 1948; that a scientist raised the possibility in March, 1949; and that a prototype airliner took to the sky in July, the reader would automatically assume a connection and settle back waiting for the new airliner to fall out of the sky. But the reader would not in reality look for such connections.

Yet a strange coincidence did develop in reality. The first de Havilland Comet — designed and built by the firm through which Shute entered aviation and about which he wrote his two journeyman novels — entered large-scale production after its success in prototype. In late 1952, five months after commercial service started, Comets began having strange accidents attributed, as in the novel, to pilot error. Between March, 1953, and April, 1954, four Comets crashed without survivors. Subsequent investigation by the Royal Aircraft Establishment revealed that the Comets were developing fatigue fractures in their wing spars but that the real cause of the midair breakups was the fatigue failure of the cabin skin that caused catastrophic depressurization. During the formal inquiry into the Comet disasters, people connected with the investigation talked about what Shute had said in his novel; and one witness is reputed to have joked, "This is a problem for Mr. Honey."

Much of *No Highway*'s appeal comes from the fact that it is narrated by an expert, the very busy young Dennis Scott with much on his mind who sits down to write Honey's story in order to relax from his own problems. Dennis Scott is hag-ridden by his own specialty, the problems of supersonic flight; and the title of a paper he gives before the Royal Aeronautical Society runs through the novel like a dark thread: "Performance Analysis of Aircraft Flying at High Mach Numbers." Honey's difficulties are resolved, but new ones take their place. Shute has supplied the happy ending demanded of most commercially successful fiction while maintaining a balance of realism: the ending is not an ending, but a way station. Most readers see the story as Honey's, not as Scott's; and they do not look beyond the end toward the ever-increasing problems brought about by the growing complexity of aviation technology. And *there* is a large part of the reason for Shute's success: he could write novels of technical interest to himself and to other engineers and present at the same time romantic adventure stories that reached large audiences of both sexes.

But the chief reason for his great success after the war, I think, was his ability to write realistic fantasies in an age crying for escape and wish fulfillment. Theodore Honey, widowed, ugly, and sallow-faced with "the features of a frog, and rather a tired and discontented frog at that" (9), comes back from Gander after wrecking the plane and finds his once messy house spotless, his homely little daughter nicely dressed, and his domestic life being run by a very pretty young woman. She is not just any young woman but a combination of the two modern mother-mistresses, a former nurse turned airline stewardess. Doubly blessed, Mr. Honey is also the object of the tender but platonic affections of a famous American movie star. This woman is not merely a concession to the clichés of the romantic best-seller, but a self-conscious comment on Shute's expanding awareness of his role as a popular writer, of his ability to touch and influence millions of readers. That the character of the actress was also a gambit easing the novel's adaptation to the screen (with Marlene Dietrich and James Stewart glamorously and effectively miscast) is merely evidence that Shute knew his genre and his audience.

CHAPTER 7

Going All the Way — Clean Round the Bend

I *Mental Flights*

"I HAVE known men of action, technical men, practical men, men who are always tinkering with machines, who yearn for a touch of the small-scale supernatural and are quite gullible in the search for it," wrote Pamela Hansford Johnson (the wife of C. P. Snow) in a review of one of Shute's last novels, *The Rainbow and the Rose*. Miss Johnson quite accurately delineated Shute's public as one "with a streak of disciplined romance and a good-humoured capacity to believe six impossible things before breakfast, if those things are allied to the power of the planchette-board, extra-sensory perception and the rest of it — white man's magic, rather light-hearted stuff, not to be taken too seriously."[1]

Although Shute did not admit to belief in the supernatural, in the significance of dreams, in extrasensory perception, in the transference of personality, or in reincarnation, all of these phenomena, and more, appear in his stories. To the question as to whether or not the former engineer was saying that "science is not enough," his late wife, a physician, replied that he would not have said such a thing but that she would have: she believed in psychic phenomena and he did not — and in this statement others close to him concur.[2] Yet, he did write many novels employing psychic phenomena, and did so increasingly as he got older. The possibility exists that this was the trick of a smart writer, a gimmick; but, because his public seems to have preferred the straight adventure or romantic story and because the mystical passages created confusion and frequent scorn from his critics, it is difficult to believe that he was not somewhat touched by a secret mysticism much in the way some of Graham Greene's characters struggle not to believe in anything beyond the mundane.

Shute's use of metempsychosis, the transference of souls, seems a

84

convenient gimmick to join the stories of characters separated in time and space, as Shute does in *An Old Captivity*, *In the Wet*, and *The Rainbow and the Rose*. And he was not above writing an occasional ghost story, though he was always unsuccessful with them, as in the very early and unpublished "Tudor Windows," a genial tale about an old house tenanted by a succession of happy couples in which the wives are always the same woman, or as in *Farewell Miss Julie Logan*, his film adaptation of a story of hallucination by J. M. Barrie.[3] What makes me suspect that solid citizen Shute harbored a need for some kind of otherworldly belief is his repeated use of the theme of the Second Coming or the advent of a Great Teacher. And, when he died, he was well into a novel dealing with a new Nativity in Australia, an epiphany he had hinted at in *In the Wet*, and one he seems genuinely to have wished as an antidote to the times.

His older daughter wrote me that she felt "he was not really 'at home' with these mystical ideas, and that he did not believe them, which is why they did not go over very well. They were intriguing ideas of other peoples and religions, in which possibly he would have liked to believe, and *might* have done had he been introduced to them earlier."[4] In any case, he knew such interests or longings were not to be expressed in his own person; and for this reason he first expressed them through an obvious crackpot, Theodore ("gift of God") Honey, who seems increasingly sound by the end of *No Highway*.

An early manuscript version of that novel is titled "The Mental Fight," a title that is an allusion to "the New Jerusalem" of William Blake that Mr. Honey awaits:

> And did those feet in ancient time
>   Walk upon England's mountains green?
> And was the holy Lamb of God
>   On England's pleasant pastures seen?
>
> And did the Countenance Divine
>   Shine forth upon our clouded hills?
> And was Jerusalem builded here
>   Among these dark Satanic Mills?
>
> Bring me my Bow of burning gold!
>   Bring me my Arrows of desire!
> Bring me my Spear! O clouds, unfold!
>   Bring me my Chariot of fire!

> I will not cease from Mental Fight,
>   Nor shall my Sword sleep in my hand
> Till we have built Jerusalem
>   In England's green and pleasant land.[5]

Former chairman of the Surbiton branch of the Society of Psychic Research — the Surbiton that was the starting point for E. M. Forster's Celestial Omnibus — Mr. Honey believes that Christ had lived in England as a child and that Joseph of Arimathea, Martha, Mary, and Lazarus had immigrated to England after the Crucifixion, as did Simon Zelotes and (for good measure) Saint Paul. " 'That's why the English are the greatest people in the world and always will be, because in the beginning we were blessed by the advice and the example and the teaching of the greatest people who have ever lived' " (25). On the basis of Talmudic lore and pyramidology, Honey expects the imminent return of Christ to England and the attendant end of the world. Since Shute's fictional subject matter usually mirrored his own enthusiasms, Mr. Honey may be expressing something that personally interested Shute; but he is expressing it in terms so extreme that no one could associate the interest with the imaginative but rational writer-engineer.

With the story of the little man in *The Chequer Board* and that novel's Eastern travel, racial tolerance, and twist of mysticism, and with the story of that other little man in *No Highway* and that novel's eccentricity and still larger use of mysticism, Shute was building toward something — but something not to be found at home in England. If travel was a metaphor in Shute's work, it was also a necessity for the man. Shortly before his death, Shute referred to travel as "the raw material of the business of most imaginative writers, but the destination is relatively unimportant; the very act of traveling is the important thing."[6] To a friend, he wrote that he ran dry if he stayed at home too long; that "one has to kick oneself out of one's comfortable home and go and travel, and travel the harder the better, in order to charge up again, like a battery."[7] Even as World War II broke out, Shute had traveled to America and then vicariously in an imaginary long-distance flight full of physical and psychic difficulties. Fairly static himself during the war, he wrote about men in constant motion — on foot, in boats, in planes; but Shute then went to Burma, wrote a novel about traveling, traveled widely in America, and began a story of transatlantic flight. Finally, in late 1947 while he was writing *No Highway*, he began planning a slow flight in his own plane across Asia to Australia and back.

James Riddell, who accompanied him on the six-month flight to Australia and back (September, 1948, to March, 1949), says that Shute started on the trip with a novel in mind about commercial aviation in the East. Indeed, Shute's thick diary, or log, about the flight contains thousands of notes on what kind of flying was done and about airports, mechanics, hotels, food, transportation, prices, people, places, customs, joys, and annoyances — details that would make it possible for him to place a character almost anywhere. During a long layover in Baghdad in early October, Shute began telling Riddell about his new novel: it was to be about an Englishman who goes East and becomes a bit mad.[8] But Shute was not sure what kind of man his hero would be. A few weeks later in Rangoon, however, Shute met seventy-year-old U Prajnananda, a former British officer turned Buddhist monk, who told him that "a new Teacher would commence his teaching in about 1960 or 1970: he would be of Thibetan-Russian-Chinese stock, educated in America. He would teach mostly in California and Switzerland."[9] Riddell, who accompanied Shute on his visit to U Prajnananda, says Shute was very interested in the old man's predictions and in the manner of his conversion to Buddhism. It was probably at this point that Shute began to think of his new novel as having two central characters, an Englishman and a mystic of mixed lineage.

Ten days after he returned to England in March, 1948, Shute sat down at the typewriter and began not his mystical novel but a fairly conventional love story about an English girl who immigrates to Australia. Although the immensely successful *A Town Like Alice* was written before the long-planned "Eastern" novel, *Round the Bend*, we should consider the latter first because it is closely related to the books that preceded it and because *A Town Like Alice* seems to have been dashed off in three or four months as a kind of income insurance policy: that is, suspecting his audience would not receive a religious or mystical novel with great enthusiasm, he wrote what he himself called a "potboiler" to recoup the funds he had spent during his six months of travel. Moreover, another reason for writing a potential best-seller was that Shute was in the process of making up his mind to move himself and his whole domestic establishment to Australia. Thus, the actual writing of *Round the Bend* was finally begun in late 1949 during a period of intense change, a period when a fifty-year-old Englishman living on a very comfortable estate on the Solent Channel rejected the country of his birth, and the people and places that had long surrounded him. Like Tom Cutter, the narrator of *Round the Bend*, Nevil Shute was ready for a new life.

II   Round the Bend

The origin of the title *Round the Bend* is found in Shute's flight-log entry for February 17, 1949: "The Air Force, who have a pretty gift for ribald names, have christened an eccentric officer in Malaya 'Harpic' — 'clean round the bend.' " The allusion is to a well-known British drain cleaner and its motto. A year later, when Shute learned that *Punch*'s Brockbank had just used *Round the Bend* for a collection of motoring cartoons, he refused to change his working title on the grounds that he had written his novel around the expression. In English slang, to go "round the bend" means to become insane or at least extremely eccentric. The central characters in the novel are not actually insane, but they have become so affected by an intense religious experience that they seem, to the outside world, "clean round the bend." The novel develops an emotional commitment that Shute's fiction had been building to since the end of the war: the first draft of *The Chequer Board* had been called "The Guided Feet"; *No Highway* was "The Mental Fight"; and, when Shute began his Eastern trip, he left behind an unfinished novel entitled "Blind Understanding." One working title suggests mental aberration and the other two suggest acceptance of forces not perceivable by the mind: only after "mental fight" do we go with "guided feet" and "blind understanding" "round the bend."

"I doubt if any of my books will be read in fifty years' time," Shute remarked a year or so before his death, "but if one does live that long it will be *Round the Bend*."[10] As for what quality made a very sane and practical man like Nevil Shute Norway often refer to a story of eccentricity as his best book, the simple answer is that *Round the Bend* is his most complex, intense, and sincere effort and that it was written during a time of near personal crisis. This answer may not be very satisfactory, but is is the best one I can give besides that of another critic who has also made a full survey of Shute's work: "He must have always been searching for some synthesis of religion which would satisfy his intense feeling for progress and his love of technology. In *Round the Bend* he provides such a synthesis, a religious movement based on the love that goes into good work . . . and the reader can feel how passionately the author believed in what he had to say."[11]

Round the Bend is the only novel Shute wrote that opens with the adolescence of a central figure or that gives even more than passing significance to the youthful development of an important character. Shute, who later rushed through the story of his own youth in his autobiography, takes unusual care in giving us the early history of Tom Cutter, the narrator-protagonist. There is little detailed background, but what Shute does give strikes me as suspiciously archetypal: the story of a very ordinary youth who goes to his first air circus and falls in love with aviation:

> They had stunt displays, and wing walking, and a parachute descent, and a pretty girl flying a glider. They had a public address loudspeaker system rigged up, and the announcer stood up once and said that Sir Alan Cobham had offered to let any pilot of the last war try his hand at flying again. A pilot dressed up as an old tramp came out of the crowd and did a bit of clowning with the announcer, and tripped over his umbrella and fell flat, and got into an Avro back to front and took it off the ground facing the tail, holding his hat on, waving his umbrella, and shouting blue murder, and went into the best bit of crazy flying ever seen in England, bellowing all the time to be told how to land it as he went crabbing down the enclosures three feet up, and the announcer bellowing back to him. My, that was fun! (3)

Round the Bend opens realistically with a description of the real air circus of the real Alan Cobham and describes on the first page one of the planes Shute had built a generation earlier, the Airspeed Ferry. And Tom starts at the very lowest level by doing menial labor in the approved Horatio Alger tradition for "young men on the make"; but this tradition was also followed by Sir Alan himself, who was "never in too much of a hurry to notice the humblest detail of his big concern" (4). Thus, one day Sir Alan offers Tom five shillings to play an eloping girl in a comic routine:

> They finished up with a Gretna Green elopement of a couple in a terrible old Model T Ford, with Father chasing after them all over the aerodrome in a Moth and bombing them with little paper bags of flour and rolls of toilet paper. . . .
> I was young, of course, and I'd got a fresh, pink and white face in those days, so I could make up as a girl quite well. All I had to do was to dress up in the most terrible women's clothes and drive about on the aerodrome in the old Ford, trying to get out of the way of the Moth. The Ford was driven by a boy about my own age, Connie Shaklin . . . a cheerful, yellow-skinned young chap with straight black hair who put me in the way of things. He was dressed up as a young farmer in a sort of smock and we did the turn together; we never turned that Ford over, but we came bloody near it sometimes. It

was good fun; we wheeled and skidded the thing all over the aerodrome, shrieking and hugging and kissing while the Moth dived on us and bombed us. The show ended, of course, with my skirt getting pulled off and me running off the field in a pair of red flannel knickers, covered in flour and with streamers of toilet paper all over me, while the crowd laughed fit to burst.

I got the five bob and Sir Alan himself said I'd done very well. *That was the first money that I ever made in aviation.* (3 - 4; italics mine)

Tom Cutter's introduction to his profession and to the man he loves is both sexual and religious in its implications: acting out a comic submission to the more experienced lad "who put me in the way of things," he begins a humble aeronautical novitiate that includes picking up trash, washing planes, and cleaning up after the passengers who have been sick in the cockpits.

Like Benjamin Franklin writing about his own youth, Cutter, who assembles a large fleet of cargo planes operating all over the Middle East and Asia, looks back with the pride of a middle-class success to his humble origins. One of seven children of a dock worker, he becomes an apprentice aircraft mechanic, learns his trade well, saves his money, buys a small twelve-year-old plane about to be thrown on a scrap heap, installs a secondhand engine, and flies to the Persian Gulf to begin a new life. Tom has learned well Franklin's way to wealth: he flies, maintains, and washes the plane, handles the correspondence and bills; and, all the while, he establishes a reputation for honesty, dependability, and frugality.

Round the Bend starts out, frankly, as a thrilling romance of business, carefully detailing Cutter's initial profits and expansion from one small plane to a second and a third, each larger than the one before. The facts and details of profit sheets, contracts, wages, maintenance schedules, licenses, bank accounts, and mechanical and personnel problems are as lovingly handled by the old managing director as a poker or bridge hand described by a master cardsman who is also a good writer. But what makes this novel different from any other book that demonstrates a careful writer's ability to interest his readers in a subject he loves is exactly the same thing that animates Franklin's *Autobiography:* both writers equate business success with virtue and thus with spiritual salvation.

Working within the Protestant ethic, Franklin gave lip service to the old Calvinist notion that good works and virtue are not sufficient without grace. For Cutter, financial success, doing good, and universal brotherhood are all closely related. On the surface, Cutter may seem to rise because he exploits "native labor," but neither Shute nor Cutter regards such employment as exploitation. Although Cutter builds his airline by employing only Arabs and Asians and although Cutter's business contacts in England regard his policy as unusual, even risky, Cutter acts upon a pilot's record, not his color or religion. The "native" pilots are cheaper, but Cutter also realizes that he will find his expansion in the East easier if he hires local crews. But Tom's hard work, his virtue, his open-mindedness are not sufficient for a major and lasting success: he needs grace or its secular equivalent, luck.

Tom Cutter's luck is his old boyhood friend, Connie Shaklin, whom he meets by chance after a thirteen-year separation and just when he needs him: "It was just like seeing a bit of light at the end of a tunnel" (78). The "light," as the reader eventually discovers, is a spiritual beacon that leads Tom out of the moral darkness created by his wife's suicide. Meeting Connie is also the light at the end of the tunnel of Cutter's steady but limited economic growth since he acquires through Connie a big transport plane on a bargain charter basis and since Connie works for him as chief ground engineer. With this bit of luck, Tom's airline makes a quantum leap, and within a few years he expands his regular service from the Persian Gulf to Australia.

As Tom's fleet and his potential worth grow, the dramatic focus of his narrative shifts from himself to his head mechanic; for Connie becomes famous throughout the Eastern aviation world as a great teacher — a prophet whose message is that "the maintenance of aeroplanes demanded men of a pure and holy life, men who would turn from the temptations of the flesh to serve their calling first" (210). In short, Connie develops an international technological credo based upon good *work*, not *works*. In his autobiography, Shute looked back on his own work on the R.100 as producing "a satisfaction almost amounting to a religious experience. After literally months of labor, having filled perhaps fifty foolscap sheets with closely pencilled figures, after many disappointments and heart-aches, the truth stood revealed, real, and perfect, and unquestionable; the very truth. It did one good; one was the better for the experience. It struck me at the time that those who built the great arches of the English cathedrals in mediaeval times must have known something of our mathematics, and perhaps passed through the same experience" (*Slide Rule*, 78). To a young pilot who asked Shute if he really believed a man could take aircraft maintenance as seriously as Connie does, Shute replied that "it was his religion."[12]

For another child of the century, Antoine de St. Exupery, flight itself
was a mystery akin to the religious experience; and, for Shute, the
sacred mystery was in what made flight possible.

The R.101 disaster and Shute's other experiences in aviation
probably demonstrated to him the desirability of a practical creed
that would bring religious fervor and altruism to an industry in
which careless mistakes could and did kill. In addition, Shute was a
perfectionist and idealist; a combination that often results in extreme
models for human conduct. Thus, it is not surprising that Shute's
first long flight in a small plane, which brought him in contact with
the laziness, sloppiness, and stupidity of countless minor officials and
service people, would lead him to create a fictional antidote. James
Riddell, whose account of the flight is required reading for those
who would understand Shute, describes "a very methodical, efficient man" with little patience for the flaws of others, and none for
his own failures, even those caused by others. Returning from
Australia, Shute was directed to land cross-wind at Brindisi; but he
lost control, ground-looped, and disabled his plane only fifteen hundred miles from England. Riddell's first reaction to the damaged
plane "was one of immense sadness for Nevil. This is *his* journey —
his plan and *his* whole undertaking. He has had all the responsibility, and it is only through his own meticulous efficiency that we
have traveled this immense distance. I know that he wanted like hell
to get back to Portsmouth on time, with an aircraft spick and span
and all in one piece."[13] Shute's obsession with careful maintenance
and flying had appeared all through his fiction from "Pilotage" to
An Old Captivity to *Pastoral* to *No Highway*. In *Round the
Bend* he went all the way and made efficiency a religious duty.

A religion that would turn Asia's ground and flight crews into
paragons of efficiency might have been wishful thinking on Shute's
part, but it was also a realistic conceit in terms of plot and thematic
strategy: such a religion would have a mode of rapid expansion; such
a religion would be appropriate in an area of the world going
through a period of intense change and culture shock; and such a
religion would share a common technical language and a common
purpose by making its message applicable to Moslems, Buddhists,
and Hindus as well as Christians.

As for who or exactly what Connie is, Shute never answers; he
keeps his prophet mysterious and avoids dogmatic quicksands. Since
most of his readers are Christians, Shute employs several common
Christian gambits: Connie (for Constantine, the first Christian

emperor) is a widow's son who begins his ministry at about age thirty among working people, lives ascetically and sexlessly, is persecuted by colonial officials, and dies of leukemia about three years after his teachings begin. After his death, his friends of different religions begin to record his sayings and the story of his life in six books, the last of which is the one before us, the Book of Cutter. Here are some reactions to Connie as gathered by St. Thomas:

[From a Hindu:] "Perhaps . . . he is just an ordinary man like you and me, who has the power to make men see the advantage of turning to God. As you have the power to make men see the advantage of sending new tracks for a bulldozer by air." (101)

[From a Buddhist:] "He has the power to make men of any religion bring that religion to their daily work upon the aircraft." (113)

[From a Christian turned Buddhist:] "Every religion in the world requires to be refreshed from time to time by a new Teacher. Gautama, Mahomet, Jesus — these are some of the great Teachers of the past, who have refreshed men's minds and by their lives and their example brought men back to Truth." (121)

[From Cutter, a nominal Christian:] "He's just a very good ground engineer with a bee in his bonnet." (231)

Shute uses Connie's convent-educated sister, Nadezna, who seems to have no creed, to explain the meaning of the new teacher. The pilgrims who come to see him before he dies, she says, do not think him a god; but they " 'venerate him as an example of what any man can attain to if he can be as wise, and thoughtful, and self-sacrificing, and as good as Connie.' " His life, in short, " 'means that God still cares about the world . . . that He has shown that care in making of one man a perfect example, to show everyone the way to live their lives out in the modern world' " (333 - 34).

Not even Connie is willing to say exactly who or what he is. When he learns he is dying, he flies around the East in a small plane setting straight the legends by simply showing himself as a man and by talking about the commonplace routines of the hangar and shop. To the very end he rejects the institutionalization of his teachings, especially when an oil-rich sheik bequeathes him millions of pounds to be used in spreading his word and in supporting his followers: " 'Great money is great power. But power has no place. in what I

teach. . . . Many evils spring from power. . . . Even from the power
to do good. . . . Either my words will last after me and be believed by
men, or else they won't' " (321). " 'Everything has now been
renounced,' " marvels one of his disciples. " 'No more temptations
can be left. This was the final one, the temptation of Power to do
Good' " (322).

Many clergymen based sermons on *Round the Bend*; but, except
for Edward Weeks who thought it perhaps Shute's best novel,[14]
reviewers were generally unsympathetic or embarrassed. Most damn-
ing was Edward Gray in the *Saturday Review:* "Connie is nothing
but a pious editorial and a vague, sweet smile."[15] I think nothing is
pious or sweet about Connie, but I concede that he might seem
vague to anyone who reads the novel as being about him. Like
Hawthorne's *Blithedale Romance, Round the Bend* is about the
teller, not the messianic figure; just as Hawthorne's early readers ignored the centrality of Miles Coverdale and his unsuccessful struggle
toward faith and commitment, Shute's reviewers missed the point
that Tom Cutter's objective is to "put down anything about my own
life that I thought would make the picture complete, and explain to
future generations why I did the things I did which ultimately
reacted upon Connie" (340).

Shute's penciled notes attached to the first draft of the novel give
us the allegorical genesis of the narrator from Saul Thomas Newman
to S. T. Newman to S. T. Cutter to Tom Cutter. As Tom grew in his
creator's mind, he became a new man acting on new principles, a bit
of a saint (S. T.), and a combination of the Apostles Paul (Saul) and
Thomas. The use of Saul is particularly interesting because it is the
name of St. Paul before his conversion on the road to Damascus and
because Shute takes several chapter epigraphs from James Elroy
Flecker's poem "The Gates of Damascus." In the novel's last words,
we are left with doubting Thomas, or Saul on the verge of conversion, still blind: "I still think Connie was a human man, a very, very
good one — but a man. I have been wrong in my judgments many
times before; if now I am ignorant and *blind,* I'm sorry, but it's no
new thing. If that should be the case though, it means that I have
had great privileges in my life, perhaps more so than any man alive
today. Because it means that on the fields and farms of England, on
the airstrips of the desert and the jungle, in the hangars of the Persian Gulf and on the tarmacs of the southern islands, I have walked
and talked with God" (341).

Round the Bend automatically invites comparison with Somerset

Maugham's story of another young mystic, *The Razor's Edge* (1944). Shute's is the more impressive novel, I think, because of its sense of involvement with the world. The narrator of *The Razor's Edge*, Somerset Maugham himself, is a witness and not an active participant. Shute's narrator, on the other hand, is from the start the symbolic wife and brother and avatar of his mystic subject. As I suggested earlier, Shute may well have started with only one character, then divided him into two "religious" men — one of the East, one of the West. Tom and Connie are both dedicated men: Tom, to the materialistic religion of wealth and the spread of Western technology; Connie, to the spiritual values of the East.

CHAPTER 8

Traveling Hopefully

I   *The Australian Trip and* A Town Like Alice

SHUTE'S longtime secretary, Mrs. Sally Bessant, says that he returned from his Australian trip, rushed through a six-month
accumulation of correspondence, and "within a matter of days he
was at work on *A Town Like Alice*."[1] The manuscript for that novel
reveals that he began it exactly ten days after returning to London in
March, 1949, and that he had finished it three and a half months
later. The speed with which he wrote this immensely successful potboiler (compared with the six months he spent on *Round the Bend*),
and the fact that a great number of specific ideas, incidents, and
characters are found in his flight log tell us quite a bit about his
craftsmanship. That he started for Australia with the rough idea for
Round the Bend in his mind, that he delayed starting that book for
eight months after his return and took twice as long to write it, and
that few of the ideas in *Round the Bend* (except for the old monk's
prophecy) are to be found in the flight log — all these facts suggest
that that novel was a far more personal and "interior" product.

The characters and incidents of *A Town Like Alice*, on the other
hand, were all shaped and suggested by the author's experiences
during the Australian trip. The novel is a very simple, economic fairy
tale: an old man dies in January, 1948, leaving fifty-three thousand
pounds (close to half a million dollars in today's terms) to Jean Paget,
a niece who does not even know him, with the stipulation that Jean,
who is twenty-seven, is to enjoy the income but not the principal until she is thirty-five. Shute's primary motive for the old man's complicated stipulation seems to be to make a place for an elderly at-
torney as narrator — and to make it necessary for Jean to plan her
ventures so carefully that even the conservative old lawyer will per-
mit her to use the capital.

With the new freedom and responsibility brought by the legacy,

Jean leaves for Malaya to have a well dug in a small village where she lived during the war; only after the well is dug, and the debt to the village repaid, does she learn that Joe Harman, an Australian soldier she believed to have been tortured to death by the Japanese, is still alive. Because she owes him a debt of gratitude (he had been crucified by the Japanese for stealing food for her and her companions), she leaves for Australia to find him. After traveling around Australia, she learns that he is in England looking for her; eventually they get together, and they marry as soon as Jean has revitalized the economic and social life of the fictional Australian Willstown and turned it into a town like Alice Springs, a real town in the center of the continent's great interior wilderness.

Shute seems to have arrived in Australia (in November, 1948) with the intention of writing a novel about an English girl who moves to that country. How else can we explain his conclusion, a few days after he arrived, that what Darwin needed was not a palatial bar, the only permanent new building being built, but a new laundry? Typically, the young woman was to be the idealized, virtuous, and resourceful heroine he had been putting into his novels for twenty years; what Shute wanted was an Australian environment and subject matter. Soon after arriving, he met one Reg McAuliffe, an insurance agent full of interesting yarns; knowing a good thing when he found it, Shute agreed to fly McAuliffe into the outback (the Australian wilderness) on his insurance selling rounds. Along the way they met a cheerful, tough station manager of about thirty-five, a man who had, as a prisoner of the Japanese, been nailed down by the hands to keep him from escaping. Shute had found the basis for the male protagonist in his new book, Joe Harman; and from not only this station manager but a doctor that he found along the way, Shute heard many stories of conditions in Japanese prisoner-of-war camps. All of this information was to go into the new novel, but much more was needed.

His travels quickly supplied him with hundreds of details that went directly into *A Town Like Alice:* the enthusiasm of Australians for things English, their attitudes toward the law, their slang — all were grist. And into his mill went such items as a bath hut over a hot water well (his heroine would bathe there), a bank manager's office infested with flies (his heroine would bully the manager into driving out the flies), a romantic coral island (his heroine would dally there and almost lose her long-preserved virginity), and a sluttish, pregnant, unmarried waitress (his heroine would show her how to make shoes). Shute investigated the flying-doctor service, the economics of water-conservation schemes, the relationships between station managers and absentee owners, the techniques of paddy dodging (the Australian version of cattle rustling), and various codes and taboos concerning the law; and all of these subjects were transformed into the plot of his story.

Within three weeks of Shute's arrival in Australia, his "moral" interests were also solidifying: "The doctor spent the morning with his patients, Reg with his insurance prospects, and I thinking what a damn shame it was that all the capital taken out of this country in the form of gold was not now available for it in water catchment schemes." In such ponderings, the doctor, the agent, and the writer were all at their respective tasks; but, a few sentences later, he tells of talking with ringers about the shortage of girls in the bleak Queensland outback. The connection between Shute's interests becomes apparant, for no money plus no girls plus no water equals no civilization.

Shute's practical mind, tempered by the demands of creating saleable fiction, began to center on the scarcity of girls: "The girls here all go off to the cities and get jobs or get married there. This is understandable, because in a place like Croydon there is absolutely nothing for a single girl to do. No amenities for her, and no job. But the boys will go where the girls are, and the future of N Queensland may lie in the provision of jobs and amenities for women" (flight log, December 15, 1948). The result was Shute's story of how Jean Paget, using the fortune left by her uncle, a fortune taken out of Australian gold fields half a century before, turned derelict Willstown into a thriving little oasis for young women and, at the same time, financed a water-conservation scheme.

Several weeks later, when halfway across Australia, Shute found his model town, Alice Springs, a mini-Chicago or St. Louis of thirteen hundred citizens, that showed "what every outback place could be, if only jobs for girls could be provided" (January 22, 1949). Within a few days, he had the mechanics of his civilization plot: "20 girls employed want a beauty parlour (2 more girls) and a fruit store and ice cream bar (1 more) and a dress shop (1 more) and a shop to buy the Women's Weekly and borrow novels (1 more) which makes 25 and so they want another girl in the ice cream bar. . . . Quite a modest employment of girls could turn Normanton into Alice Springs" (January 24).

Meeting an alligator trapper who supplied hides for English leather-goods firms made Shute ask himself why someone did not cut out the middleman by making shoes in Australia. As a result, Jean Paget starts a small shoe factory employing girls, then opens various shops to sell them things to get back the money she pays them, then finds ways to "exploit" the men attracted by the girls. As life in Jean's town improves, more girls come; as the girls come, more men come. The cattle stations expand because of the men attracted by the girls (including one man who comes after his girl with a bulldozer and stays to build dams to save water to induce the growth of the cattle population).

When the girls marry the station hands and settle down, they make vacancies for more girls and create new markets for new merchandise and services; and within three years Jean has opened a swimming pool, a beauty shop, an open air cinema, a laundromat, a dress shop, and an ice cream parlor (with separate but equal facilities for the aborigines). Between having children herself, Jean makes plans for a grocery and a household store. There is even talk of building a good paved road to the nearest rail point so trucks can get in more easily with all the supplies Jean's closed economic system needs. This summary indicates the storyteller's dreamy simplification and acceleration of the complex and slow process that turns out-of-the-way frontier settlements into stable and attractive communities.

The day after Shute jotted down the details about a girl-explosion, he and Riddell left Alice Springs on their return trip to England. By this time, he had most of his basic story; but he lacked a really powerful focus to make it more than just a story about a girl who goes to Australia and builds a small city. From the station manager who had once been nailed down by the Japanese and from the doctor who had also been a prisoner of war he had received some fascinating stories; he had plenty of background for his male characters, but what about his heroine? As we have seen, things tended to go well for Nevil Shute; and in this instance, an earlier kindness was rewarded: after passing through Sumatra in November, he had sent a copy of *No Highway* to a Dutch official who had helped him through visa difficulties; when this official heard that Shute and Riddell were passing through again on their way back to England, he arranged for them to spend the night with the family of a refinery manager:

Geysel is a man of about 40, his wife about 26 - 27 with two children. A slight, cheerful girl who looked as if she had led a very sheltered life. Both had been taken by the Japanese in 1942. The husband was put in a camp at once. The wife, aged 21, with her 6-months old baby, was herded about Sumatra with 80 other women and a large number of children. They were given no clothes and little food: the Indonesians supported them. The Japanese passed them from town to town; they stayed nowhere more than a few weeks. In 2-1/2 years this girl walked 2000 kilometres, 1200 miles, carrying her baby. Practically all the other women and children died. She came out fit and well, and retained her sense of humor. (February 10, 1949)

This material provided the rest of the story: Jean Paget was to spend the war wandering around Malaya with an orphaned baby on her hip. Shute, having met Mrs. Geysel-Vonck and having in his mind the image of a cheerful young woman carrying a baby, gave his own heroine someone else's baby; and he based upon that prop infant Joe Harman's mistaken notion that Jean was already married and his explanation of his failure to search for her immediately after the war.

A Town Like Alice is such a typical product of Shute's talent for writing best-sellers that a summary of the stages of its creation is in order. When Shute arrived in Australia, he knew only that he wanted to get a story out of his visit; but he did not know what or where his story was. A series of chance acquaintances led him to spend several weeks in the Gulf of Carpentaria region of Northern Queensland; and the more time he spent there, the more likely he would devote a novel to that area — but what would the novel be about? Spending several days in Alice Springs just before he left gave him the answer and the title: write about how to bring a town like Alice Springs to Queensland. But who exactly would his heroine be? Passing through Sumatra, he met her prototype. When he got back to England, he turned on the novel-writing machine in his head, started with a chapter set in England, and then began to play the tape of his memories backward. He started with a group of three chapters set in Indonesia; then a chapter in Alice Springs (where Jean meets a girl named Rose and learns the possibilities of what can be done in the line of making an attractive town in Australia); finally, still traveling backwards, the story settles in Northern Queensland where it had originally started in Shute's mind.

Once he had his basic story straight, half the job was done. The other half was finding the right narrator: by choosing an elderly lawyer as his storyteller, Shute was able to provide a constant professional commentary upon Jean's schemes and indirectly to instruct the reader how to feel about them. But the narrator is more than an index to Jean's fiscal soundness: he is secretly in love with her, which helps make her more attractive in the reader's eyes, and he comments upon the meaning of the story. When his partner calls Jean's legacy a trivial affair, the old lawyer disagrees: " 'I'm beginning to think that this is the most important business that I ever handled in my life' " (296); it is, in short, "no small matter to assist in the birth of a new city" (305).

II *How to Write a Best-Seller*

I referred two paragraphs earlier to Nevil Shute's novel-writing machine — now let me suggest how the machine worked. Shute gathered ideas and impressions; jotted down notes on possible titles, names, character traits, time sequences, distances traveled, individual lines, chapter endings, last sentences, key themes, bits of poetry for epigraphs, and other materials; and then one day began writing. If he could get past the first chapter, he usually had a novel — for the first chapters gave him the most trouble. As his own accounts and his manuscripts show, he frequently rewrote the first chapter several times. Otherwise, he generally wrote his books through from start to finish, composing directly on the typewriter, single-spacing the lines, and leaving a wide margin for corrections. As he finished each page, he opened a drawer, placed the page inside, and closed the drawer, thus keeping his working surface neat. When he arrived at the last page, he put the finished draft aside for a week or two before making corrections. He rewrote very little beyond the first chapter, a habit which gave his books a good deal of spontaneity.

The overriding impression we get of Shute's working habits is a sense of his discipline and regularity. He wrote from nine o'clock until one, "every morning, seven days a week, except one Sunday in the month when I go to church."[2] His secretary says that "he did not approve of people who suddenly made up their minds to 'Write for an hour or two' at any time of the day or night."[3] The result was occasionally mechanical as in *A Town Like Alice* where the chapters were all the same length until Shute got well into his story; but the books got written. Indeed, all the gimmicks and tricks of the popular novelist's craft worked; for *A Town Like Alice* became a tremendous best-seller, was serialized in women's magazines, and was filmed. Shute had set out quite calmly to write a book that would appeal to a large audience in order to "pay" for *Round the Bend*, which he thought would be a commercial failure — which it was not. He set out to write a book full of hard work and happy adventure that would provide escape for his rather disspirited fellow citizens in those drab years just following the war. He made Jean Paget a mirror of the novel's ideal reader, the kind of young woman who likes "novels with a happy ending . . . paintings that were a reproduction of something that she knew" (26). He knew his audience; for, when he signed copies of *Alice* in a Melbourne department store, at least half of the four hundred women who flocked to buy it were young secretaries and clerks. We might carp that no normal woman would send a telegram exactly like the one Jean sends Joe ("HEARD OF YOUR RECOVERY FROM KUANTAN ATROCITY QUITE RECENTLY PERFECTLY DELIGHTED STOP" [161]), but normal female readers did not seem to mind.

The critical reception of *A Town Like Alice* was however, predictably unenthusiastic. To the *Commonweal* reviewer, the fifty-three thousand pound legacy so overwhelmed the plot and characters that the money became the hero;[4] *Time* found Jean "as unconvincing as a Horatio Alger hero";[5] and the *Times Literary Supplement* suggested that "Mr. Shute, with his high moral purpose and happy ending, is perhaps reminiscent of the nineteenth-century didactic novelist, or the contemporary Soviet Russian writer whose aim is to 'improve' reality rather than to merely reflect it."[6] These reviewers were correct, but they overlooked the fact that Shute set out to do just what they accused him of doing. Just as the *Commonweal* reviewer charges, Jean's inherited money is a kind of hero in this novel, and much of the excitement comes from the implied question of whether or not she will do something of value with the legacy. In Shute's middle-class protestant view, the question is one of almost religious impact, analogous to the parable of the ten talents. Jean rejects the lawyer's suggestion that she live on the interest and devote her life to working without pay for a charitable organization: " 'Surely, if a thing is really worth while, it'll pay' " (25). Wealth must flourish, else it would not come to us.

The "message" of *A Town Like Alice* becomes clearer if we look upon that novel as a training exercise for the economic mysticism of *Round the Bend.* For both Tom Cutter and Jean Paget, material success is a metaphor for salvation — which may explain the fascination of the old lawyer-narrator, who is on the verge of death, with aiding in the wise employment of Jean's legacy. The narrator's Christian name, *Noel,* may be meant to suggest the formal or sacramental nature of his role. What happened, I think, is that some of the enthusiasm Shute was saving for *Round the Bend* may have influenced the content of *Alice.*

A decade later Shute was to write that "Most people seem to think *A Town Like Alice* is a good book although I don't, but it reflected my first views and experiences of Australia."[7] Though he spent only two months in Australia, and though there is no record of his meeting any Australian writers or reading any of the country's literature, *A Town Like Alice* seems a very sensitive rendering of the Australian experience, not just Shute's. "Classic" Australian literature is full of outcasts and criminals; and Shute treats two polite versions of these Australian archetypes: Jean, condemned to wander about Malaya; Joe, nailed to a tree and beaten for stealing a Japanese officer's chickens. The central dramatic action of the novel's last portion deals quite well with the rescue of another station manager who has come onto Joe Harman's property to steal young calves, some of which Joe stole from him earlier; and the friendly and illegal competition of these men, though totally alien to Shute, is attractively presented. We find in this same rescue scene not only hints of Australia's rather brutal past as a convict colony, but common Australian themes of mateship, of isolation, and of the impact of the landscape upon its inhabitants. "Literary" Australians and station managers might have found it presumptuous of Shute to write *A Town Like Alice*, but most Australians were flattered that a well-known English author had not only chosen to write about them, but had done so with sympathy while giving many hundreds of thousands of readers in England and in America their first detailed impressions of Australian life.

III   *Moving to Australia*

Shute claimed his initial desire to visit Australia came from looking at old maps of the continent on which fences and huts were indicated in the vast expanses of an otherwise empty land: "There was all that white space on the maps . . . and right in the middle of Queensland there would be a small dot marked 'hut.' I began wondering how it would feel to be a man living in that hut in the midst of the Australian outback."[8] A continent to catch the fancy of a highly imaginative man who had spent his life on a crowded and well-mapped island, Australia also recommended itself as a country that the English-speaking world would like to read about. His travels in America the year before he went to Australia showed him nothing that had not already been well covered; in fact, the only parts of the New World that seemed to interest him at all up to this point were the wastes of Greenland in *An Old Captivity* and the Canadian wilderness in *No Highway*.

But being interested in a country as a subject matter does not usually cause a fifty-year-old man who is well encumbered with the material rewards of a successful life to pick up and move halfway round the world. As to why Shute did so, the answer most frequently given is social and economic: "He saw all the original acts of the Labour Government as stultifying to the initiative, designed to stifle the kind of technological creativeness he himself represented, designed to level down to mediocrity by legislation, rather than to elevate to freedom and better living by adventure and competition."[9] Moreover, Shute's extremely high taxes as a successful writer not only provided welfare for people he did not want to help but discouraged him from writing as much as before. Of the eighteen thousand pounds he expected to make from *A Town Like Alice*, he would be able to keep only about three thousand in England against close to fifty-eight hundred in Australia, which at least had a Conservative government at that time and a remote possibility of lower taxes.

Also contributing to Shute's dissatisfaction with England was a series of outwardly petty problems and incidents. Servants were hard to get, and life was generally quite different from before the war. He was unable to obtain sufficient petrol for his automobile under the rationing laws, and his appeals to officials proved fruitless. Shute was a world-renowned author who had done his part in the war; who had devoted fifteen years to the growth of British aviation; whose books were bringing tens or hundreds of thousands of American dollars into England at a time when England needed them. To do his work, Shute needed enough automotive petrol to travel around England to gather details for future books to earn future dollars; and he was, moreover, willing to exchange his surplus aviation petrol allowance for automotive. None of his logic worked; he was told, in effect, not to ask for special treatment.

Politically, Shute might best be termed a "democratic elitist." He believed in the basic or potential equality of men, he believed in the value of social mobility, but he also thought that hard work should bring tangible economic and social rewards, that the man who does more for society than his neighbors should enjoy greater privileges and advantages. When he abandoned England, he made his reasons so public that a question was asked in Commons about his "mistreatment." Moreover, Shute's move was wrenching for his family that was being shifted from a country house surrounded by five acres of gardens and lawns running down to a tidal creek on the

Solent to the unknown. "I was called home from boarding school
and told that we were leaving our house in Hayling Island," his
older daughter said. "I thought we would be moving to somewhere
else in Hampshire, but I was told '*No. Australia.*' The idea appalled
me. But I couldn't say anything. It was like that with dad. It was no
use arguing. He had made his decision."[10]

Shute's reasons for leaving England should not be seen as entirely
negative. Shute was not so much running away from one country as
toward another. Australia was a good place to be in 1950, for it
offered an egalitarian society in which extraordinary achievement
was encouraged, recognized, and rewarded; it was a popular country
for a popular writer; and it was a country that offered subject matter
as potent as that of James Fenimore Cooper — the civilization of a
new land. But, most important, Shute's first visit showed him that
"to live in Australia in the next twenty years will be a great adventure. It will probably be for me the last and greatest adventure of my
life and that, I think, is the chief reason why I have come here to
live."[11]

<h3 style="text-align:center">IV   The Far Country</h3>

Shute finished *Round the Bend* in May, 1950, while his household
was being packed around him; and early that summer the four
Norways, Mrs. Bessant, and the family gardener-handyman sailed
for Australia. They settled temporarily in a rented house about thirty
miles south of Melbourne — in the part of Australia that most closely
resembled England in landscape and in climate. There, on the
Mornington Peninsula, Shute was able, as in England, to keep a
boat; and he had a tremendous country to explore with Item Willie,
his well-traveled plane. For eight months, probably the longest
voluntary break he took from writing during his professional years,
Shute got to know his new country and to search for a permanent
home for his family. After writng two novels in one year between a
gruelling trip and the pulling up of old roots, he deserved a vacation
— but, with typical regularity, he asked his publishers to withhold
publication of *Round the Bend* for six months longer than necessary
so there would be no long gap between that novel and the next one.

When Shute finally sat down at his typewriter in March, 1951, he
wrote *The Far Country*, a pale copy of *A Town Like Alice*. Ignoring
what had made *Alice* interesting — the prisoner-of-war chapters and
Jean's one-woman, rural renewal project — he wrote a conventional
love story. In it, Jennifer Morton comes to Australia from England to

visit her aunt and uncle on their wool station; meets a Czech refugee, a former doctor now working as a lumberman; falls in love; and decides, after some conventional vicissitudes, to marry him and to settle in Australia. Shute claimed he wrote one novel for himself and one for the public; so just as *A Town Like Alice* was a potboiler preceding *Round the Bend, The Far Country* was another paving the way for the "serious" novel that he began later that year, *In the Wet*. A comparison of the relative merits and future of life in England and Australia, *The Far Country* reflects Shute's dissatisfaction with his old country and his enthusiasm for the new; having made up his mind, Shute proselytizes for Australia directly (though he also quietly criticizes Australia's poor handling of talented European refugees).

Where Jean Paget had gone to Australia because nothing held her in England and because she loved an Australian, Jennifer Morton is made to reject positively Labourite England. But the rejection of England is not a rejection of the English character and English ideals, which are alive, the novel suggests, in Australia. Jennifer's ancient grandmother, looking back at England as it was, and Jennifer's father, looking ahead to an even bleaker future for England, arrive at the same conclusion: Jennifer should go to Australia.

Jennifer, usually annoyed by her enthusiastically Socialistic coworkers in the Ministry of Pensions, has to watch her grandmother die of genteel malnutrition because her pension, as the widow of an upper-level civil servant in India, ceased with the granting of Independence " 'when the Socialists scuttled out' " (50). When Granny dies, Jennifer tries to put aside the temptation to join her aunt in Australia by thinking of all the beauty and "history" England has to offer. But, as she ponders, "two devastating little words came into her mind — So what?" (101). As a result, she almost magically exchanges the dreary English winter and its drearier shortages for the bright Australian summer and material prosperity. She spends her first day in Australia with her aunt and uncle, sheep farmers on a modest scale, who have received a twenty-two thousand pound wool check and have come to Melbourne to meet Jennifer and buy a few things. That they are free to spend thirteen hundred pounds in one day, more than most Englishmen earn in a year, and that no restrictions and rationing exist impress upon Jennifer the message that Australia is a blessed land where hard work provides a good life, where an abundant middle-class existence is still possible.

Is Shute materialistic? The question is irrelevant: he is simply mirroring a world in which the attainment of wealth and material rewards had always been one of man's chief goals — and the goal of nations. Thus, Shute looks upon Jennifer and the other new Australians as subsidies given Australia by England and Europe. By allowing her to emigrate, England has given Australia the value of Jennifer's nurture and education; Europe has given the value of the medical education of Carl Zlinter, the male protagonist (or should I say "costar"?).

The Far Country is definitely a minor production, but it is as carefully engineered as any novel Shute wrote. The theme — the renewing power of a new land — is tied closely to the plot: a first chapter tells how Jennifer's Aunt Jane, encouraged only by her Aunt Ethel, left England after World War I to marry an Australian sheep-man, how they prospered, and how they decided to send five hundred pounds to Aunt Ethel, Jennifer's grandmother. The second chapter introduces us to Jennifer and disposes of old Aunt Ethel but not before she gives Jennifer most of Jane's check. After this chapter, we have a heavily propagandistic one in which Jennifer decides to go to Australia; a chapter set in Australia before Jennifer's arrival that introduces us to Carl Zlinter, the doctor-lumberman, and ends with his discovery of a fifty-year-old tombstone with his own name and birthplace on it; then a chapter devoted to Jennifer's arrival in Australia that ends with her going for a ride on a heavily timbered mountainside:

> It was lovely sitting there in the car. . . . She stretched luxuriously in her clothes. It was quiet in the forest, or it would have been, but for the distant and rhythmic rumbling of a bulldozer at work.
> She sat listening to the bulldozer. . . . The noises repeated in a regular cycle; a roaring acceleration of the motor followed by a few seconds of steady running, then a period of idling. . . . It varied very little; she sat listening to it dreamily, half-asleep in the coolness of the forest.
> The cycle was disturbed, and woke her from her doze. A rumbling of heavy timber broke in and the roaring of an engine mounted suddenly to a climax, and then stopped dead. There was a noise of tumbling machinery and a continued rumbling of rolling logs; a few men shouted in the distance, their voices puny and lost among the greater noises. Then everything was quiet again. (159 - 60)

I've quoted this passage at length for its sleepy, relaxed quality; having established his basic characters and ideas, Shute creates a dreamlike respite at the exact center of the novel before he slams everything together. The sound that pulled Jennifer out of her dream was the crash of logs and a bulldozer falling on two lumber-jacks. Within minutes of the end of her dream and the end of her past, she has met Carl Zlinter and is assisting him in amputating the leg of one man trapped under a bulldozer and then helping him with a delicate operation upon the crushed skull of another.

From there on the story becomes almost pure fairy tale, for Jen-nifer finds in herself a vitality she had not known in England and Carl recovers from the long years of war as a battlefield surgeon in the German army and the longer years of internment after the war. Together, they search for the identity of the "Charlie Zlinter" whose grave Carl found; and Carl eventually discovers that Charlie, who was once celebrated in local song and legend for drowning while drunk, left behind a small cache of gold — enough to pay for a year of medical study so he can be licensed to practice medicine in Australia (the emergency operation was illegal). No, the resolution of the plot is not very probable, but it is the kind of poetic justice Shute strove for in his potboilers: just as Jean Paget revitalized Willstown with the profit her ancestor took out of the Australian gold fields, Carl gets to practice medicine legally for the greater good of Australia because of another golden legacy from an ancestor who had gone there before him.

CHAPTER 9

Looking Forward — And Back

I Getting Settled in Australia

The Far Country was a happy, optimistic book written by a man who had, on the surface at least, found a large amount of fulfillment and contentment. Shute was pleased with his new country, and many Australians took pride in the fact that a successful English author had chosen to live among them and create attractive images of their land. " 'Nothing uppish about him like other pommies [transplanted Englishmen] around here,' " said an Australian neighbor. " 'Fights the bushfires and comes to the agricultural shows just like the other fellows.' "[1] In spite of a mild heart attack in 1951 that caused him to give up flying his own plane, life went on in his new home much as before. When he encouraged old friends to come to visit him, many did; and visiting literati, such as A. P. Herbert, stayed with the Norways. Close by them lived Ian Hassall who had worked under Shute during the war; a painter born the same month as Shute, Hassall had come to Australia a year or so earlier and was already becoming known as an interpreter of Australian scenes and characters. Alec Menhinick, another navy friend, soon joined them.

In mid-1952, Shute moved into a large new brick house in Langwarrin. Behind the main house was a small house for the two girls, and the main house itself contained the usual formal and family rooms, guest rooms, a study for Shute, an office for his secretary, a darkroom, and a workshop for his machine tools. Early in 1952 he described his surroundings in a letter: "I have bought about one hundred acres of land, mostly rundown pasture and scrub in rather a beautiful situation about thirty miles south of Melbourne on a hillside looking out over mountains and sea. We are very busy and will be for the next five or six years turning this into a decent grazing property. At present I am running twenty-four Aberdeen Angus cat-

109

tle on it. . . . I employ three families on this acreage, two of them being migrants from England and one an Australian family."[2] Over the
years, he joined together three farms, increased his herd of cattle,
and added pigs. The farm failed to make a profit, but he liked working around the property, doing small jobs, playing at gentleman
farmer.

He could afford to lose money, for his books were bringing in ever
greater earnings. When he arrived in Australia, his total literary earnings, after agency commissions, for his first twenty-four years of
publishing came to 121,933 pounds (sterling). But from 1950 on he
equalled that sum every few years: in fiscal year 1951 - 1952, he
earned over 32,000 pounds (Australian), and in the following year he
topped 40,000; by 1959 his tax bill (not his income) was 39,-
037.6.10 pounds.[3] Such an income suggests that Shute had become
one of England's two or three best-selling writers by the time he
moved to Australia, and he was being called the "Prince of
Storytellers." In short, he was such an established figure by 1950
that his English publishers issued a standard edition of his novels, including the out-of-print books published in the 1920s and 1930s. He
had thought *Round the Bend* would be a critical and financial disaster, but his American publisher said in several letters that he
thought it the best thing Shute had done; and many appreciative
letters about the novel arrived from clergymen, including several
bishops. When *Round the Bend* showed signs of being the biggest
commercial success in Heinemann's history, one member of the
publishing house wrote him that, "If 'the Incomparable Max' [Beer-
bohm] was still wielding a sprightly brush, what a cartoon he could
have made — yourself in the middle surrounded by Galsworthy,
George Moore . . . and all the others."[4]

Such success must have eased whatever small pains settlement in
the new country may have caused. By and large, the move seems to
have been a liberating experience for Shute. In *The Far Country*, for
example, not only did he sprinkle his characters' speech with rude
terms like "bastard," "bloody," and "mucking well pissed," but he
deigned to speak about the subject of art, something he had never
done before, in an entertaining passage in which a rich grazier and
his wife search through Melbourne's art galleries for a "nice" painting and find things by one artist who "had modelled his style upon
that of a short-sighted and eccentric old gentleman named Cézanne,
who had been able to draw once but had got tired of it; this
smoothed the path for his disciples a good deal." Another artist is a

primitive, "unable to paint or to draw, and hailed as a genius by people who ought to have known better." The man and his wife find no painting to their liking, and they buy instead a new utility vehicle — "a very lovely motor car, a low, flowing dark-green thing with more art in it than anything that they had seen that day" (127 - 29).

Though incapable of masquerading as a literary man, Shute began to lecture about writing — about the joys, problems, rewards, and duties of the professional writer. In England, where he felt himself a stranger in the literary and artistic world, Shute had remained generally silent on such matters; but, in Australia, a country just beginning to be interested in culture, he wrote and lectured on the importance of trusting one's own likes and dislikes in both art and literature. At the opening of an exhibition of paintings by Ian Hassall, he presented, for the first time publicly as far as I can tell, his aesthetic credo:

> I sometimes think that in writing a book the fundamental decision that an author has to make is this: is he writing to please himself or to please other people. If you write to please yourself you may turn out a wonderful piece of literature that students will still be reading in a thousand years from now, but let there be no hard words if people don't spend their money on it in your lifetime, because it wasn't written to please them.
>
> I think the same decision must be made by the artist, and that is why the work of Ian Hassall appeals to me so much. Here is an artist who works not to please himself with esoteric colour forms and symbols, but to please other people. . . . A disciple of Holbein, of Burne Jones, and of Orpen; unfashionable names, perhaps, but men who strove to make their art an opening of the horizons and a source of pleasure to people who don't know very much about it.[5]

This was the creed of a popular artist or writer, which is exactly what Shute was and all he wanted to be.

Again and again, starting in 1951, Shute asserted that material success was necessary to the creative writer to keep him writing — but such success had to come from the reading public, not from prizes or fellowships or grants: "Too much encouragement from literary authorities without corresponding support from the public may induce in the writer an illusion that he is a superior person to the common man, and a belief that if the public will not read the pearls of wisdom that he lays before them they should be made to do so in their own interest. From this attitude of mind arises a belief in totalitarian government, whether of the fascist or the communist variety."[6] Rejecting the elitist view of the writer, he strove to present himself to the local Rotary Club as a simple craftsman of words and ideas who could proclaim that "an author is paid by the world according to the job he does for the world."[7]

As to why the world had paid him so handsomely, he admitted to friends that he put many attractive characters in his books so readers could find someone with whom to identify; and to a stranger he wrote "sincerity is the first attribute for *making money* in the *business* of writing novels."[8] But neither of these attributes — sympathy or sincerity — provides us with an answer. Though he generally dismissed his tremendous popular success as the simple good luck of having a knack for writing, he tried in his Rotary Club speech to give businessmen a practical answer that they could grasp — it was all a matter of supplying a market with a service: novel readers seek ethical guidance, books sell well when they help readers solve problems, but writers must avoid sermons, since "the function of the entertainer is to entertain." To his fellow Rotarians he described his readers as residents of "a perplexing world, beginning to think and wonder what it's all about, what to do for the best. What entertainment do such people want?" For one, they want information based upon research, the kind of factual information he presented in *Round the Bend* and *A Town Like Alice*. For another, they like a love story "because people in love are normally clean and brave and self sacrificing, at their best." Then come "stories of heroism and self sacrifice, of people battling through against difficulties, particularly modern difficulties." Finally, such readers want a "happy" ending, even if it entails death; they want "guidance to victory, not to defeat."

II In the Wet

An analysis of Shute's first seventeen novels shows that they all conform to this four-point program: information, love, heroism, and a happy ending. Novel number eighteen, *In the Wet*, which was begun about a month after the Rotary Club speech, uses all four devices and adds an often used fifth: topicality. The writing of *In the Wet* began in November, 1951, while Australia was preparing for a royal visit. Late in 1949, George VI had begun to plan a trip to Australia and New Zealand to take place in 1952. As it was to be the first visit of a reigning English monarch, there was naturally much interest in Australia. But, late in 1951, the king had to cancel his preparations because of an operation, and it was announced that Princess Elizabeth was to make the royal visit in his place.

Thus in November, while Princess Elizabeth was in the middle of a very successful tour of Canada, Shute began a novel dealing with her decision as queen, some thirty years in the future, to leave England to its dreary Labour government and to divide her time between royal residences in Canada and Australia.[9] At the end of January, 1952, Elizabeth and Philip began their trip to Australia when word came of the king's death on February 6. Within three and a half months of George's death, Shute had finished the first draft of his novel[10] which was not published until May, 1953, a month before the new queen's coronation and eight months before her tour of Australia.

It is difficult to say just how *In the Wet* grew in Shute's mind. Was the book inspired by the forthcoming royal visit? Did nostalgia for England cause him to write about the queen, the symbolic head of the Commonwealth? Or did Shute's general interest in the future of Australia and his pessimism about England combine with topical interest in Princess Elizabeth and her Commonwealth tour? The king's death, which came when Shute was in the middle of the writing of the first draft, did not spoil his story since it was set in the distant future anyway; but the king's death did, I think, help force the story into a rather symbolic, even mystical, track by reminding Shute that, though the king may die, what he stands for lives on in his heir.

A synthesis of the Christian and Buddhist motifs that Shute had employed in *Round the Bend, In the Wet* opens with the death of a "godless" old man named Stevie during Queensland's wet season. (When Shute's British publishers objected to the obscure Australian expression as the title, Shute argued that setting the novel's frame "in the wet" season gave rational readers an acceptable explanation for an apparently implausible story, since "certain events or hallucinations can happen in the unusual and feverish atmosphere of the rainy season."[11]) Attending Stevie on his deathbed are an old Chinese Buddhist and the narrator, an old Episcopal priest. As Stevie lies dying, animals gather outside in a "semi-circle round the house, their heads all turned in our direction, watching. The cattle were there, and the wild dogs, and the dingoes, and the wild pigs, and the wallabies" (47 - 48). To the old Buddhist, the animals represent the reincarnation of other spirits. The Christian narrator, however, is less certain: " 'I suppose they've been attracted by the light' " (48) and

"I didn't see why the death of one drunken, dissolute old man should excite the animal kingdom very much" (50). The Nativity-like conduct of the animals should not escape the careful reader, however, nor should the fact that Stevie's fatal illness begins on January 6, the Feast of the Epiphany. Shute's reason for beginning the novel with a set of references to Christian and Buddhist beliefs and traditions is not made clear until the very end. Rather than spoil Shute's effect by explaining too much at this point, let me call the reader's attention to *In the Wet*'s epigraph, which Shute took from a hymn he had sung as a youth at Shrewsbury School:

> Lord God of Hosts, through whom alone
> A Prince can rule his nation
> Who settest Kings upon their throne
> And orderest each man's station;
> Now, and through ages following,
> This grace to us be given:
> To serve and love an earthly King
> Who serves our King in Heaven.[12]

As Stevie dies between dark and dawn, he dreams or hallucinates that he is a thirty-year-old pilot living in the year 1982. This "dream" (which makes up the bulk of the novel) is "passed" to the narrator, who is holding Stevie's hand and is apparently receptive because of a recent bout with malaria. The pilot's name is David Anderson and he is Queen Elizabeth's pilot as the Commonwealth approaches 1984. Outside of being called "Nigger" by his friends because he is a quarter aborigine, David seems to be a perfectly ordinary romantic hero. Yet, strange things keep happening to him: while stopping over at *Christmas* Island during the queen's flight from Canada to Australia, David dreams he is an old man dying in a dirty bed; and on *Christmas* day on another flight from England to Australia, he saves the queen from assassination. Otherwise, the story of David seems to be just a romantic vehicle for Shute's speculations about the future of England and the Commonwealth. Chiefly, Shute purveys through David the notion that the queen must take a more active part in the affairs of the main Commonwealth nations. By the end of the novel, the queen has settled safely in Australia and has left in England a governor general who forces the Labour government to resign and brings about electoral reform.

Exhausted after the long flight on which he saved the queen,

David falls asleep while thinking about his fiance, Rosemary, whose name suggests the traditional symbol of remembrance. Asleep, he dreams once more that he is an old man dying in a hovel "in the wet" surrounded by animals; as he dies in the dream, he mutters "Rosemary." At this point in the dream within a dream, the elderly narrator awakens and goes to the door and looks out to discover that "the wild dogs and the wild pigs, and the cattle, and the wallabies stood in a circle round the house in the grey, rainy dawn, their heads all turned to us in adoration, watching the majesty of his passing" (314).

Four months after the death of Stevie, the narrator is called upon to baptize a baby born to a shepherd named Jock Anderson and his half-caste wife, Mary. The baby, to be named David, was born at the very hour of old Stevie's passing in January, 1953 — thus, he appears between the death of the old king in 1952 and the coronation of the new queen in June, 1953. The reader is left to assume that this Epiphanal child will grow up to be the pilot who protects the queen thirty years later (David's baptism on May 11, the feast of St. Philip, seems a tribute to the royal consort). The many Christian symbols surrounding David's birth (born among animals to a mother named Mary, etc.) are not meant to suggest a Second Coming or a Messianic role but to establish a ceremonial relationship. That is, Shute is honoring the queen and her position in the Commonwealth by evoking divine references, allusions, and imagery to buttress her symbolic position.

But what exactly was it that made Shute, a proponent of social mobility and a constant admirer of the "little man," sufficiently a Royalist to proclaim in a speech that "We cannot have a Queen and not be ruled. We must accept our Queen into our country and give her her rightful place in our political life with some small sacrifice, perhaps, of carefree independence"? The answer, that the crown helps protect citizens from the bungling and stupidity of bureaucrats and politicians, is found in the same speech:

. . . there is one last resort when civil servants get too stupid and create injustice; any man or woman can sit down and write a letter to a King. . . . I sat down once myself in blazing indignation on behalf of an old lady who had suffered great injustice from officialdom and wrote a letter to the King, spilling the beans. It worked immediately; within three days a close investigation of the case and of myself was taking place; within a fortnight the

red tape was cut in pieces. I discovered later that I was one of the very many
people who have done this thing and seen injustice righted.[13]

From his airship days, bureaucrats and politicians had been
Shute's *bêtes noires*; and he never shied away from attacking the
beasts. Thus *In the Wet*, set in George Orwell's dreary 1980s, por-
trays a dispirited England full of empty houses deserted by owners
who have fled to Australia and Canada. The only growing British
institution in this vision of a Labour government run amuck is the
civil service. In a debate in the House of Commons soon after
Shute's death, a Conservative member linked Shute and Orwell as
writers who had influenced public opinion against Socialism. The
speaker, Charles Curran, claimed that Shute, "in 30 years of writing,
had achieved an almost unique ascendancy over a new section of
society, the nonprofessional middle class. Mr. Shute could almost
have been called 'the Dickens of red brick.' "[14]

Shute had done more, however, than bait the Labour mentality
that had driven him away from England; for he had argued very per-
suasively for a multiple-vote system that would allow the educated
and the successful a greater voice in elections. Starting with a
universal basic vote, he proposed a second vote based upon education (a university degree); a third on foreign travel (earning a
living outside Australia for two years); a fourth for raising two
children to age fourteen without getting a divorce; a fifth for
achievement (" 'It's supposed to cater for the man who's got no
education and has never been out of Australia and quarrelled with
his wife, but built up a big business' " [98]); a sixth (appropriate
to the novel's religious bias) for being a minister of a "Christian"
church; and a seventh given at the queen's pleasure. Shute would
have automatically rated the first five votes, of course.

Surveying postwar English novelists, Robert Greacen found them
"wary of taking sides; they understand, partly instinctively and
partly from their everyday experience, the importance of social class
in their own society, but they will not write thesis novels. . . . they
want to reflect their society rather than change it. The signs are,
however, that the old class divisions are melting at the edges, and
that Britain is getting ready to move forward, though reluctantly,
into a scientifically based, meritocratic society."[15] Unlike the
novelists described by Greacen, Shute took sides gladly and delighted
in writing thesis novels that would help engineer change. Having

spent his formative years in a young industry in which ability and practical results were cherished above birth and seniority, Shute seems, with C. P. Snow, in the vanguard of the literary apostleship of meritocracy. This apostleship began for Shute in the 1920s with his Stenning books, and it culminated in the figure of "Nigger" Anderson, who, born in the wilderness, played tennis with the queen of England ("Royalty defeated the common clay six three, six four" [208]).

Although Shute seems to have enjoyed writing *In the Wet* and although its sales were good, the novel was poorly received; indeed, it incurred more critical wrath than any of his other books. As a young writer, he had shrugged off adverse reviews; now, as a staple of the publishing industry, he struck back in a curiously defensive speech entitled "On Stirring up Hornets Nests":

> Most book reviewers would no doubt prefer to earn a comfortable living by creative writing,but have not been gifted with an interest in the matters which interest the reading public. Their appreciation of the art of writing makes them valuable as critics of that aspect of literature and here they are appreciated by the public. They are less valuable as critics of the ideas contained in that literature.
>
> On the lower levels of literature, the immature books and the books that do not present any very controversial ideas, the reviewer probably guides the public well. At the extremes the divergence is most marked. The book which thrills the reviewer with its artistic perfection will probably not be accepted by the public, while a book which the public value for its contents will probably seem trivial and worthless artistically to the reviewer, or even offensive and in bad taste.[16]

III   *Writes Autobiography*

Slide Rule, subtitled *The Autobiography of an Engineer* but signed by the novelist, deals with his life up to the time of his departure from Airspeed in 1938. His original intention was to call this book "A Journey to Australia" and to end it with his reasons for leaving England;[17] but, having attacked postwar Labour policies rather heavily in *The Far Country* and *In the Wet*, he had probably become bored with the topic. Moreover, as he told an old navy friend, "I think that one should see things in perspective and stop an autobiography at least ten years previous to the date of writing."[18] The most likely reason for his curtailment of the autobiography is that he lost interest. Despite his dislike for editorial meddling, he wrote his British publishers in February, 1953, when he was about halfway through the first draft, that it might be very long and that he would not mind its being cut as the publisher wished. He seemed so genuinely disinterested in his own life story that he sent a long memoir about his days with the Department of Miscellaneous Weapon Development to Gerald Pawle, who was writing a history of that organization, and invited Pawle to make whatever use he wished of the material.

Though even the *New Yorker's* review was favorable, though *Slide Rule* has interest as a concise indictment of the bureaucratic and political folly that had weakened England as an air power between the wars, and though it is a competent study of why some fliers live to a ripe old age and others die stupidly, the book is a disappointment because it stops short of the most potentially interesting years of his life — World War II and his growing success as a novelist. In addition, more than a third of the book is a superficial reworking of a long-forgotten article he had published twenty years before concerning the airship scheme to which he had devoted six years of his young life. When a law firm investigated at Heinemann's request the airship portion of the book to prevent possible libel suits, the lawyers made recommendations for changes; but Shute, who rejected most of them, explained that the events were so far in the past and that so few of the people involved were alive or involved in engineering that there would be little chance of a lawsuit. However, Shute never mentioned that his subjects had had a chance twenty years before to bring suit against him; he presumably did not want to call attention to his use of old material with little alteration.

IV   Requiem for a Wren

That Shute was tired of writing or that he might have been afflicted with failure of the imagination is shown by his beginning, soon after he finished *Slide Rule* in mid-1953, to rework a novel he had left unfinished five years before when he set out for his first visit to Australia. The unfinished novel, "Blind Understanding," was itself a reworking of the ideas in a short novel ("The Seafarers") Shute had written immediately following World War II but had never published. The result of this rewiting was the darkest novel Shute had yet written — *Requiem for a Wren*, a story *by* a man who had set his own records straight *about* a man who sets straight the record of a young woman who has committed suicide.

To trace the growth of *Requiem* through its several stages, we must consider the use Shute made of his earlier fiction. "The Seafarers," a happy little novel of the women's magazine variety, was written in 1945 or 1946, and is an attempt to carry romantic wartime yarns into peace. Donald Wolfe, a young torpedo boat commander, and Jean Porter, a rating in the Women's Royal Naval Service (Wrens), return to dull civilian lives and drift apart. But they both get involved in reconditioning old boats, meet again in nautical surroundings, form a business partnership, make a terrific profit on their first joint venture, and resume their courtship under the aphrodisiac of financial success. Such escapism was fine for the war years when spirits had to be maintained, but something else was needed in the grim postwar years.

Shute put "The Seafarers" aside and wrote *The Chequer Board* and *No Highway*, but he returned in March, 1948, to the story of young people who make an adjustment to peace. This time, however, he saw the dramatic possibilities of dealing chiefly with a young woman's problems in returning to civilian life and in coming to terms with wartime experiences. As a result, he built, "Blind Understanding" around how Janet Payne, the genteelly reared daughter of an Oxford semanticist, became an Ordinance Wren servicing Oerlikons, the antiaircraft guns Commander Norway's department had helped introduce. In this novel, Janet Payne — a direct descendant of "The Seafarers" Jean Porter and an ancestor of *A Town Like Alice's* Jean Page — is a happy, practical young woman who takes pride in her marksmanship with the Oerlikon.

At first elated when she shoots down a German plane, she is unhappy when she learns that the plane was carrying Hermann Behnke, her father's old student and assistant. A German national, Behnke had been working for the Allies as an agent in Germany; Janet's guilt over having killed him and the other agents in the plane becomes obsessive when she begins to regard the later deaths of her fiancé and her father as punishments for her pride. The basic story line had some merit, but Shute cluttered it with an almost Gothic accretion of plot and counterplot. After the war, a young Oxford scholar named Prentice begins to delve in Janet's father's notes and manuscripts. He learns, by chance, that Hermann Behnke was involved in a plot to assassinate Hitler (which Janet seems to know already) and that the plot was really a German General Staff scheme to negotiate a peace that would have left Germany strong enough to continue the war later (which Janet did not know). The rough draft ends abruptly with Janet about to go aboard a motor launch with a pair of sophisticated gunrunners while some kind of gigantic conspiracy simmers in the background.

Whether or not Shute abandoned the story for good or simply set it aside when he left for Australia in 1948 is unclear, but the story seems to have stayed in his mind, perhaps because some of the central dramatic scenes in "Blind Understanding" — such as the futile attempts to rescue a man trapped in a flooded tank or the seven bodies in the ruins of a German bomber that was built to carry a crew of four — were based upon incidents he had witnessed in early 1944 and had reported in his unpublished Ministry of Information articles. These incidents had worked on the imagination of the novelist; they were not the kind of scenes he could forget; for, when he was finished with looking back at his life in *Slide Rule*, he utilized almost without change the wartime experiences of Janet Payne in "Blind Understanding" and turned them into the experiences of Janet Prentice, the heroine of *Requiem for a Wren*.

Narrated by Alan Duncan, a fairly normal man teetering between two worlds on dummy feet (his real ones were shot away in the war), the novel opens with Alan's belated homecoming in 1953 at the age of thirty-nine to his parents' huge Australian sheep ranch. His parents' only surviving son as well as a lawyer, Alan is a middle-aged, middle-class heir apparent — a slightly flawed Prince Charming in a fairy-tale setting and situation. His father's house, built by Alan's original-settler grandfather (also named Alan) in the style of Queen Victoria's Balmoral, is a brick castle. Not all is well in this little kingdom, however: the new parlormaid has inexplicably killed herself.

To make short work of a heavy story, let me suggest that *Requiem for a Wren* is about order itself, and that the death of "Jessie Proctor" tests all Alan has learned at Oxford and in chambers, tests his ability to take the reins of "a small rural community . . . led by wise and tolerant people such as my father and mother, staffed by good types culled and weeded out over the years" (44-45). Instead of resting after his long journey, Alan spends his first evening at home searching out possible motives for the parlor maid's suicide, fearing she may have killed herself because of "some evil that had grown up with the aging of my father and relaxation of the firmness of control." Alan finds the dead girl's hidden suitcase and opens it because he feels himself "responsible for the happiness and well-being of everybody in our little community so far as lay within my power. Amongst our little party there had been enormous, catastrophic grief that had made this girl take her life. Unless I knew what it was that grief might come again" (54 - 55).

In the parlormaid's suitcase is a diary identifying her as Janet Prentice, the former Wren he has been searching for since the end of the war. Janet Prentice's diary tells the same story Shute had set out to tell about Janet Payne in "Blind Understanding": how the daughter of an Oxford semanticist shoots down a German plane carrying seven defecting airmen and descends into debilitating guilt. When Janice Prentice learns of the death of her fiance (Bill Duncan, Alan's younger brother) and later of her father—killed in Normandy by two sky-larking German girls who were having fun with a mortar—she becomes a self-proclaimed scapegoat, atoning for her generation's war guilt. She had enjoyed the war, enjoyed messing with boats and guns; but she begins to believe she has done something for which she must be punished. "God looks after that," she writes in her diary,"and it's fair enough, because if you kill seven people wantonly just to show how good you are with an Oerlikon you've got to be made to suffer for it" (232-33).

To an interviewer Shute explained it was extraordinary that no one seemed to notice that *Requiem for a Wren* was the same story as *A Town Like Alice*, "one with a happy and the other with a tragic ending."[19] An obvious reason for the similarity is that Shute wrote *Alice* on the rebound from the unfinished "Blind Understanding," which later become *Requiem*. In each novel, an English girl seeks in Australia a man she knew during the war while the Australian is busily searching for her back in England. Until *A Town Like Alice's* Jean Paget goes to Australia in search of Joe Harman, "she had never really recovered from the war. . . . She lived, but she had very little zest for life. Deep in the background of her mind remained the tragedy of Kuantan, killing her youth" (149).The major difference between Jean Paget and Janet Prentice is that Jean finds she is needed in Australia whereas Janet learns that her dead fiance's elderly parents, whom she had hoped to help with her modest inheritance, are wealthy sheep ranchers.

Though Janet finds contentment in acting under an assumed name as parlormaid in the house of which she was once meant to be mistress, she kills herself because she is afraid to confront Alan Duncan. Not knowing that he has been searching for her for years, not knowing that he secretly wishes to marry her, she seems afraid that he will reject her and even more afraid that he *will not* — that he will want to marry her and that she will taint him with her guilt. For him to marry an extremely unbalanced young woman in his own slightly unbalanced condition would be, in Shute's eyes, madness. Her suicide clears the record for him, leading to a probable marriage to a healthy young woman waiting in the wings.

In Shute's view, Alan Duncan and Janet Prentice are trapped by a concatenation of events and no serious blame will accrue whether they fail or succeed. As a younger writer, Shute had preached sermons from time to time, but he soon learned that though the common reader wanted advice and guidance, he did not want sermons. So Shute took an engineer's approach to writing fiction; he developed a simple cause and effect story line. "Most people," he told a gathering of businessmen, "do not realize that if they do certain things certain results will follow. The craft of the novelist is to show them, and to conceal his message deep in the substance of a first class story."[20] By beginning with Janet's suicide, Shute throws the dramatic interest on Alan, who perceives that "in some way that I did not want to understand, I was responsible for her death" (224). Had Alan not been obsessed with self-pity after the war, he might have been able to help Janet; moreover, had he told his parents of her existence, they would probably have recognized her when she sought them out under an alias. But Alan did not tell them because he felt guilty about not having done something earlier to help the girl his brother had loved.

In spite of the depressing subject matter, the novel ends on a positive note. From the dead girl's diary, Alan learns how much the sheep-hands, who all live on the estate, count on him to marry, settle down, and carry on his father's work. So instead of punishing himself or running away, he goes into the bathroom connecting his room with his dead brother's, takes off his artificial feet, and gets into a warm tub. Tired after his long journey and a sleepless night of finding and then reading a dead girl's papers, Alan prepares to wash away his old confusion and ignorance, to soak until "I came to my senses and the power of reasoning put out emotion from my mind" (280). Newly baptized, he gets out of the tub and dresses "for my new life," exchanging his dinner jacket of the night before for a grey flannel shirt and "the brown-green trousers of a grazier" (281). Then he places a call to that sensible girl in London, and while he waits for the call to go through to his sane queen-elect, begins to tell his father why the parlormaid killed herself.

With more care, *Requiem for a Wren* could have been one of Shute's best novels. As it is, it remains a very trite book with touches of greatness in it. Those touches, however, leave the perceptive reader dissatisfied with the total work. There is, for example, the description of the arrival of Janet and another young Wren at their new station, a requisitioned country estate: "all afternoon the two girls wandered up and down woodland paths between thickets of rhododendrons in bloom, each with a label, with water piped underneath each woodland path projecting in stopcocks here and there for watering the specimens. They found streams and pools, with ferns and water lillies carefully preserved and tended. They found a rock garden half as large as Trafalgar Square that was a mass of bloom; they found cedars and smooth, grassy lawns" (84). Having obviously established an Eden for Janet, Shute then gives her free will to accept or reject the Edenic existence: "Here in this lovely place upon the Beaulieu River there was no war, and at first practically no work; *if she had chosen to do so* she could have spent most of that summer sitting in the sun in the rose garden reading poetry" (85). Instead, she gets involved in the work of the station. Her willingness to do more than is expected of her leads inexorably to her shooting down the German plane full of defectors one bright spring morning. Each man, Shute seems to be saying, finds his own original sin, his own way of falling out of Eden.

CHAPTER 10

The Death of Man

BY the time Shute finished *Requiem for a Wren* in 1954, he had a much more universal fall in mind: the destruction of mankind itself by nuclear war. The basic idea for what would become *On the Beach* grew out of the wishful thinking then current in Australia: that radiation from a nuclear war in the northern hemisphere would be held above the equator by the trade winds. Shute's first intention seems to have been to write a kind of modern Swiss Family Robinson about the continuation of civilization in Australia. In fact, Shute had discussed in his 1952 speech before the Victoria League the advantages of locating Commonwealth guided missile design and production in Australia. The chief advantage, of course, would be the influx of highly trained engineers and their families that would not only add to the industrial potential of the country but also make Australia "a great deal safer from invasion than we are now."[1]

The idea for the book "started as a joke," Shute told a friend. "Now that I was living in Australia I kidded my friends in the northern hemisphere, telling them that if they weren't careful with atomic explosions they'd destroy themselves and we Australians would inherit the world."[2] "The idea stayed in my mind in that form for about a year, in a slightly cynical and humorous form," he wrote an interviewer; but, when his research showed him that Australia would not escape nuclear doom, "it became an attractive speculation — what would ordinary people in my part of the world do with that year? A book was clearly emerging. . . ."[3]

I *Preparing for* On the Beach

Early in 1955, to keep busy while planning the major new novel, Shute wrote *Beyond the Black Stump*, a slick little fiction dramatizing the confrontation between Australian and American characters and culture. This new novel clearly developed as a result of Shute's groundwork for *On the Beach*, for he was planning to center the big new novel around an American survivor and an Australian girl. Because he had never before depicted a major American character, Shute, the careful craftsman, set out to learn about Americans at first hand. As a result, he stayed with the family of Doctor C. L. Gilstrap in Oregon for three weeks and traveled into the Rockies on horseback. This trip to America (in September, 1954) had been preceded by a six-week visit to West Australia where oil had been found, and his interest in Australian petroleum exploration may have been based on his assumption that oil was an obvious prerequisite if civilization was to flourish in Australia after total war in the northern hemisphere had cut off regular supplies.

With typical economy, Shute put together the two trips and built his new novel around a young geologist from Oregon who meets an Australian girl during a survey for oil on her father's million-acre sheep station. Even before he went to America this story seems to have been vaguely formed; for, just before he left for Oregon, he wrote his American host about the trip to the Australian West: "the country is very desolate and this small pocket of American and Australian oil drillers are having a very interesting social influence on a very desolate and backward part of the country."[4] And, when he had finished his stay in Oregon, he summarized his projected story in the course of thanking his hostess for the chance to compare her married son's life "with that of similar young . . . people in England and Australia" and to examine "the differences between your life and ours."[5]

Later, Shute was anxious that the Gilstraps not consider themselves as being pictured in the book; for, though many small incidents and details came directly from his visit to their home and community, the novel relied heavily on common American stereotypes. The American protagonist, Stanton Laird, is an extremely competent but dull young man who neither smokes nor drinks; he begins every other sentence with "surely"; he travels with the Bible and a portable ice cream freezer; and he is followed around the world by the *Saturday Evening Post*, " 'a very remarkable magazine' " that, according to a well-educated Australian, " 'never ought to be allowed outside America' " (202). Seduced by peach ice cream and glossy magazine advertisements as much as by the young American, the Australian heroine, one Molly Regan, goes to Oregon with Stanton to meet his family. But cultural shock occurs when

Stanton's family and neighbors, though they consider themselves frontier types, are unable to accept the genuine frontier irregularity of Mollie's background: she is more or less illegitimate and has half-caste siblings. Mollie returns to Australia to marry the boy next door (next door being a good thirty miles away), and Stanton presumably settles down in Oregon and marries his old high-school sweetheart.

Although *Beyond the Black Stump* is a formula situation comedy with little of the comedy, the very fact that it was composed soon after Shute's exposure to an American family and to its automobiles, gadgets, magazines, and evenings with television makes it valuable as an outsider's reaction (even if stereotyped) to *homo Americanus* during the Eisenhower years. Stanton Laird differs from another contemporary English view of the American character in only one essential: Graham Greene's "quiet American" did not live to bring his girl friend home to his parents. Although Stanton Laird is upright, sober, and materially generous, he is a hollow man, a moral and social vacuum to whom "nothing was very real . . . that did not happen in the United States" (22). Stanton may be a type, but he is an accurately drawn one. Even when he kills minor characters for the sake of the plot, Shute does so with a fine eye for American traits: Stanton and his best friend accidentally kill one of their girlfriends in a jalopy tag-game when they are only sixteen; thirteen years later, the best friend flies his Air Force jet into a locomotive while committing a practical joke.[6] The rough vitality of Americans; the latent violence of their adolescent and their adult games; their goodheartedness, optimism, and obsessive sense of fair play — all of these characteristics would appear a year later in *On the Beach*.

Beyond the Black Stump is a weak but fascinating novel because it betrays Shute's serious, unresolved questioning of values he had long accepted. Specifically, the work is that of an engineer who seems to realize for the first time that the technology he had espoused all his life might not be capable of creating an earthly paradise. If Stanton Laird and his home town are the fruits of industrial wealth, Australia should reject the industrialization that Shute had predicted and had welcomed only a few months earlier in speeches and in interviews. At that time, he had asserted that "[Australia] is a country with everything before it. It's what's called an expanding economy. Every time you drive along the road to town you see a new factory going up. It gives you a kind of kick to see that."[7] In his first Australian novel, *A Town Like Alice*, he had espoused rapid growth and affluence. Now, he seems to be saying in *Beyond the Black Stump* that Australia is the last frontier and that it would be folly to kill it with the questionable boon of coast-to-coast "civilization." The result is Shute's first almost static novel: the American oil-survey team finds no oil; the Australian girl forgets her romantic daydreams and goes home; the geologist quits his job. The sense of movement, change, and expansion that had marked Shute's earlier books is now aborted and is soon followed by an almost motionless story of waiting for the end of mankind.

A few years before *On the Beach*, Shute wrote that "When I was a student I was taught that engineering was 'the art of directing the great sources of Power in Nature to the use and convenience of man.' "[8] But in *On the Beach* he began to contemplate the *abuse* of those great sources of power. He began, in short, to take the position of his old mentor in the 1920s and 1930s, Sir Dennistoun Burney, who believed "there is the great danger that the world will not understand what science has given to it, and, just as a child may play with danger, not realizing and not understanding what he is doing, so the world may play with war and unloose such forces as will produce another dark ages."[9] As an engineer with a strong imagination, Shute could balance and evaluate theories about what nuclear war would mean; therefore, when he concluded that all life might possibly be destroyed, he could not write a dishonest story about the continuance of civilization in the remote "safety" of Australia. His quest for knowledge darkened him, for it had shown him a universal fate.

It could be that Shute was also disturbed by continuing trouble with his heart. In November, 1955, shortly before he started writing *On the Beach*, he was hospitalized in London with a minor heart attack. But the real trouble, I think, was not a heart attack but a change of heart: the end of the affair for the engineer and his machines. He had spent most of the 1930s helping to develop techniques that were to have great military value (the retractable landing gear and in-flight refueling, for instance); his war years had been spent on new instruments of destruction; in *Requiem for a Wren* he had begun to examine the psychological dangers of using tools of war; and then he turned in *Beyond the Black Stump* to the logical cultural extension of the religion of efficiency: absolutely dull young men do their jobs very well without worrying about whether particular jobs will be successful, worth doing, or "moral."

On the Beach envisions a world destroyed by gadgets, but this world still loves the gadgets which have destroyed and will outlast their makers. The best example is the cataclysmic auto race that comes late in the novel; although "nobody worried very much about the prospect of a car spinning off the course and killing a few spectators. . . . Few of the drivers were prepared to drive straight into a crowd of onlookers at a hundred and twenty miles an hour. Racing motorcars are frail at those speeds, and a collision even with one person would put the car out of the race" (241). Round and round the track goes mankind; it is concerned only with proving that one machine is faster than another; therefore, it is concerned more with the efficiency of the machines than with the safety of the men who use them.

But Shute is not mocking man; he is only explaining how things are. In fact, he bought a brand new Jaguar XK 140 when he started writing *On the Beach* and raced it himself in order to write about racing in the novel — or that was his excuse. And the character with whom he most obviously identifies, his physicist-spokesman John Osborne, devotes his last weeks to winning the world racing championship; he then puts his Ferrari on blocks, carefully preparing it for eternal storage, before taking a suicide pill in the driver's seat. As radiation poisoning becomes general at the novel's end, an American submarine captain takes his submarine out to sea and sinks it, crew and all, in international waters rather than leave it behind unprotected. Meanwhile, back on the beach, a young woman watches the submarine until it is lost to sight; then, in the novel's last sentence, she "put the tablets in her mouth and swallowed them down with a mouthful of brandy, sitting behind the wheel of the big car." Drug, drink, car — these things are the best the world has to offer. Shute is not criticizing; he is only saying that man seems unable to reject the creations of his machine culture.

II   On the Beach

On the Beach has more mood than plot, and this mood illustrates T. S. Eliot's vision of the Hollow Men that Shute chose for his epigraph:

> In this last of meeting places
> We grope together
> And avoid speech
> Gathered on this beach of the tumid river . . .
>
> . . . .
> *This is the way the world ends*

> *This is the way the world ends*
> *This is the way the world ends*
> *Not with a bang but a whimper.*

Shute was so far removed from his old dramatic plotting that he asked his British publishers not to use a representational dust jacket. "If a pictorial one is necessary, I would incline to a scene of the main four or five characters standing together quite cheerfully highlighted on a shadowy beach of a shadowy river — the Styx."[10]

The last meeting place of the characters is a suburb of Melbourne, the southernmost major city in the world and the last to be affected by the radioactive dust cloud blanketing the rest of the world. The characters who meet are Dwight Lionel Towers, captain of an American nuclear submarine; Moira Davidson, a young Australian, Shute's most liberated woman (she drinks too much, talks like a fishwife, but never manages to bed Dwight Towers, who is still faithful to his wife back in long-dead Connecticut); John Osborne, the racer-physicist; and Peter and Mary Holmes, a typical young married couple who are included as a mirror for Shute's usual readers. The story relates how they wait for death through the Australian summer, fall, winter, and spring of 1962 - 1963 (manuscript notes indicate the novel had been started with the provisional title "The Last Year").

In whittling the subject of the end of the human race down to size, Shute had decided to center his story on people who live in a small suburban sea-side town like his own. He started his novel, therefore, with the young family man Peter Holmes (an avatar of 1939's Peter Corbett) and found a way to have him discover a dying world. For that reason, the novel opens with a dramatization of the basic attitude of all the characters through Lieutenant Commander Holmes who awakens with a sense of happiness that puzzles him until he remembers this is the day he gets a new duty assignment. He has been "on the beach," and he wants to do nothing more than to work — like all the other characters, he plans to keep busy until the end.

Not until the third page do we even know that there has been a war, and even then not what kind or of what degree. Instead, we are simply told there had been a short war and that it had ended a year previously. As Peter Holmes gets dressed, we learn the war lasted for thirty-seven days in 1962 and that no history of the conflict and little record outside of seismographic readings exist. That there can be a war without a history, a war measured only on seismographs, is such a chilling understatement that no more information is needed.

Shute quietly demolishes the optimist's prime argument against the possibility of total nuclear war: that man is too rational to destroy himself. Speaking of man collectively, Shute admits such a belief might be true; but his view is that nuclear weapons increase the power of the minority of irrational men. Thus, the novel has someone, no one knows exactly who or why, drop a hydrogen bomb on Tel Aviv. When the British and the Americans make a demonstration flight over Cairo, the Egyptians retaliate by bombing Washington and London in Russian-made bombers with Russian markings. With the nations' statesmen dead, the British and American military unleash their bombers on Russia before the Egyptian ploy is discovered. The horror of this scenario is that the responses to the first provocation were rational to the extent that they were based upon the accepted military reasoning of the time. Once the bombs started falling, they fell until they were all used; in Shute's eyes, the great folly is not in using the bombs but in having had them in the first place.

Careful not to criticize anyone, Shute makes Commander Towers a sympathetic and reasonable figure; and he has him state that, had he been in control of the bombs and missiles, he would have used them down to the last one once the war had started. To Shute, order, obedience, and organization are the foundations of civilization and the prerequisites of ideal existence; rational men like Dwight Towers should not be asked or expected to violate that order simply because to destroy mankind is immoral. Instead, the novel cautions that civilized men should not place themselves or their leaders in the position of having to make an either/or choice between disobedience and destruction.

In the late 1950s, Stanley Milgram, an American psychologist, set out to find statistical support for the thesis that something was inherently "wrong" with the German character. In preparing for going to Germany, Milgram tested his procedure in New Haven to establish a norm. When he found that it was an extremely simple matter to induce apparently normal subjects to administer what they believed to be strong electric shock to an unwilling "victim" (an actor, though the subjects did not know this) who pretends to pass out from the agony of the shocks, Milgrim decided he did not need to go Germany.[11] Disturbed at first by the ease with which the subjects had been induced to commit an act against their will and the mores of their society, Milgrim later concluded that obedience to some form of authority and order, even at the cost of harming others, was an absolute requirement for the maintenance of civilization. This same conclusion had been reached by Shute long before Milgrim made his.

On the Beach's message, if any, is that human society was a nice try; unfortunately, it worked too well, trundling down the path until it found a way to destroy itself. It is not the novel of an angry, or even an anxious, man; it is that of a man who has seen the possibilities and accepted them. Mankind endures in obedience only, making its appointed rounds, going about its business as usual. If a thousand rockets have been launched, why not launch the rest? Dwight Towers floods and sinks his submarine with all the crew aboard when the men begin to show signs of radiation sickness — after all, if they die ashore with the boat in dock, no one would be left to safeguard that piece of highly classified military property. That no one would be left, anyway, makes no difference to Towers.

There is something both awful and wonderful about the way life goes on quite normally in *On the Beach* as the characters wait for the radiation level to rise. The almost total lack of sensationalism, of corpses, and of ruins makes the horror stronger. And the blandness of the characters caused annoyed reactions such as this from Colin Young: "in a tale of what purports to be nothing less than the end of our civilization, Shute's treatment inevitably results in flatness, tedium, in a lack of urgency, where above all what is required is a vivid representation of the differences between people."[12] If that "vivid representation of differences between people" is required of Shute, then why not of T. S. Eliot, whose "Hollow Men" supplied so much of the tone of the book as well as the title? Camus organized *The Plague* around a large cast of extremely diverse characters because he wanted to show how different people reacted in the face of a common disaster; but Camus' characters did not share a common fate, whereas Shute's do. According to David Martin, they await a universal death that "brings to the surface not individual complexities but the human archetype"; and, for Shute to have followed Camus' lead, Martin continues, "would have produced a work more interesting than *On the Beach*, but probably much less effective with the great public; weaker as a social document and as propaganda, less memorable in the long run."[13]

Many reviewers were made uncomfortable by the way Dwight Towers keeps talking of his wife and children in Connecticut as though they are alive, and of the presents he buys to give them when he returns home. But Towers' fidelity and sense of homecoming is logical in so far as the condition of mankind has undergone a massive change. Except for a relative handful, those who were living are now dead — and the land of the dead has become the real world, the permanent world. Only the world of the living is transitory; for all the farmers harrowing their fields, all the housewives planning their gardens, and all the doctors operating on patients to give them a few more years of useful life know, intellectually, that they will be dead in a matter of months or weeks. But the man in our without-end real world who plants a tree knows he will not live to see it mature. How soon death will come is completely relative. Besides, as Jack Turner says in *The Chequer Board*, " 'All be the same in a hundred years.' "

The story of Jack Turner is worth remembering: Turner's stoicism and his discovery on the verge of death that all men are basically the same marked the beginning of Shute's long road to *On the Beach*. Moreover, Shute's idea of sending a dying man around the world to discover his own meaning prefigures the two long voyages of Commander Towers' submarine. The voyages of U.S.S. *Scorpion* (named for the reputedly self-destructive arachnid?) keep the otherwise static story moving physically to Queensland and then to the West Coast of the United States. Voyages of discovery, they show that man's universal fate is death. Shute sends his characters "travelling hopefully" again: " 'Even if we don't discover anything that's good,' " says Towers of an impending voyage, " 'it's still discovering things. I don't think we *shall* discover anything that's good, or very hopeful. But even so, it's fun just finding out. . . . Some games are fun even when you lose. Even when you know you're going to lose before you start. It's fun just playing them' " (73). To Moira Davidson, who wishes to be dead because she finds life " 'like waiting to be hung,' " Towers replies, " 'Maybe it is. Or maybe it's a period of grace' " (47).

Shute's stoicism, remarkably similar to Hemingway's, leads me to a natural comparison: *On the Beach* employs the same basic metaphor for death as *Across the River and into the Trees* — in each case, Eliot's "tumid river" has to be crossed by characters who wait for death. Hemingway's Colonel Cantwell dies quietly in an automobile, as do several of Shute's characters. Knowing that Shute read very little fiction, I am sure he was in no way influenced by Hemingway's novel; but they somehow arrived at similar characters and situations because both novels deal with American officers waiting for the end in foreign lands and because both officers are involved in platonic affairs with younger women and act more as fatherly tutors than as lovers.

" 'That's the way it is,' " says Towers of the death that awaits him, and " 'We've just got to take it' " (48, 144). Nothing else can be said or done, for the world's death has no meaning, is simply a result, a consequence. Man is not even asked to accept it, for it lies beyond acceptance or denial. Unlike Hemingway, however, Shute did not deny his characters the ability to take death on their own terms: where Hemingway's Robert Jordan, Harry Morgan, Colonel Cantwell, and Thomas Hudson (of the posthumous *Islands in the Stream*) wait for death, none of the major characters in *On the Beach* let death take them; they take it instead. So subtly does Shute handle the suicides, so gently and naturally, that none of the reviewers seem to have noticed that *On the Beach* is a novel about suicide. No one dies a natural death; no one dies of radiation poisoning; and, of the five major characters, Moira, who most felt the pain of waiting, waited the longest.

III *The Success of* On the Beach

In spite of Shute's certainty that *On the Beach* would be a commercial failure, that not even his most faithful readers could easily stomach a book saying hard things about man's immediate future, it quickly became his greatest financial and critical success; moreover, when it brought him yet another wave of readers, the novel supported his observation that "books written with a purpose tend to be financially more successful than the purely entertainment books, because they are invariably sincere."[14] The novel's obvious sincerity has kept it alive and so has its versatility. It has been praised and taught by pacifists, theologians, philosophers, political scientists — and it now appears on "environmental" reading lists.

Indeed, *On the Beach* may well be the first important fictional study of ecological disaster. When Moira asks if scientists can do anything to stop the radioactive dust that is drifting down to the southern hemisphere, Towers answers, " 'Not a thing.' " " 'It's just too big for mankind to tackle. We've just got to take it.' " Moira rejects her fate as unfair, for " 'No one in the Southern Hemisphere ever dropped a bomb. . . . We had nothing to do with it. Why should we have to die because other countries nine or ten thousand miles away from us wanted to have a war?' " (48). Shute had discovered Spaceship Earth for himself, and probably did more than any other writer or thinker of the 1950s to make a large audience understand that men must suffer equally the results of what they do at home or allow to happen far away. Moreover, the novel's stylistic stoicism and objectivity make for an absolute sincerity that left the burden of responsibility on the reader, and made it clear to him that the novelist did not care one way or another how he reacted. After all, " 'It's not the end of the world,' " says Shute's alter ego, the auto-racing scientist. " 'It's only the end of us. The world will go on just the same, only we shan't be in it. I dare say it will get along all right without us' " (97).

When Shute had dipped into the future a few years before in *In the Wet*, he had justified his excursion with the postscript claim that "unless somebody makes a guess from time to time . . . we are drifting in the dark." Because he has an admiring audience ready to give him a hearing, the popular writer has power, Shute later observed, and is in the best position to make such guesses and to "play the part of the *enfant terrible* in raising for the first time subjects which ought to be discussed in public and which no statesman cares to approach. In this way, an entertainer may serve a useful purpose."[15] Since Shute wrote these words the day before his death, we can take them as his final thought on the subject of the novelist's role.

Philip Wylie, another writer very talented at looking at the future, suggested that *On the Beach* "ought to be compulsory reading at the Pentagon, West Point, Annapolis. Ike [Eisenhower] should set aside his western and puzzle his way through it."[16] But Shute was not writing for presidents and generals who already knew about the possibilities of nuclear war. When I came across a letter from then Senator John Kennedy that thanked Shute's American publishers for sending him a copy of the novel, I wondered for a minute whether or not he would have dared the Cuban Missile Crisis had he read *On the Beach*. However, I returned to reality when I thought that presidents do not need novelists to tell them what can happen — they already know, or are supposed to. Moreover, Shute was talking to the ordinary reader, to the man charged with the extraordinary responsibility of telling his politicians what to do.

And when I read John Kennedy's letter, I suddenly remembered that 1962, the year Shute chose for Armageddon, was also the year of the Cuban Missile Crisis. And if the contemporary reader quivers a bit when he remembers that Shute's nuclear war grew out of the Arab-Israeli conflict, he also recognizes that Shute has once more seen the future.

CHAPTER 11

The Death of Nevil Norway

I The Rainbow and the Rose

JUST as Shute regarded the death of man calmly and dispassionately in his fiction, so also did he look upon his own death. During the war, when John Rowland published a mystery entitled *The Death of Nevill Norway* (1942), Shute marched into the outer office of Rowland's publisher in full uniform and demanded to see the head of the firm. When the receptionist, surrounded by demonstration copies of *The Death of Nevill Norway*, asked whom she should announce, he got his laugh by startling her with his firm reply: "Lieutenant Commander Nevil Norway." To Shute, danger was a joke: "I suddenly went crazy the other day," he wrote a friend a few months after his November, 1955, heart attack, "and ordered an open two-seater Jaguar XK 140 so you will probably see my obituary notice before so very long."[1] He had taken up road racing, feeling that he had reached the age when he was calm enough to do so, that he had lived his life and learned something of patience.

With the completion of *On the Beach* in late 1956, Shute seems to have entered an autumnal period not quite of retirement but, in retrospect, the highly definable period of a mature, confident writer who has said his piece and can relax. Though he had usually written a novel a year since 1938, he finished only two books — *The Rainbow and the Rose* and *Trustee from the Toolroom* — in the three years he had left to him. They were gleaming books, serious but not evangelical; not morbid, but rich with memory and the promise of youth replacing age. This promise he began to fulfill spectacularly in a third novel ("Incident at Eucla") begun two months before he died, for this novel dealt with the Second Coming of Christ in the form of a baby born in the Australian wilderness.

Shute took the title for *The Rainbow and the Rose* from a line in Rupert Brooke's "Treasure," a poem celebrating the speaker's

hope that, even though his senses may die with age and deprive him
of the sight of the rainbow and the scent of the rose,

> Still may Time hold some golden space
> Where I'll unpack that scented store
> Of song and flower and sky and face,
> And count, and touch, and turn them o'er
> Musing upon them. . . . (ii)

The story revolves literally around an unpacking of memory: a
middle-aged pilot sets out to rescue the aged pilot who taught him to
fly thirty years before and, in the process, begins to relive his own
and (through dreams) the older man's life. Writing *The Rainbow
and the Rose* was also an exercise in nostalgia for Shute, for it
returned him to his oldest subject matter, aviation, which he had not
touched upon in detail since *Round the Bend,* the last novel he wrote
while in England. Aviation had a strange power over him as he admitted in the very last words of his autobiography: "once a man has
spent his time in messing about with aeroplanes he can never forget
their heartaches and their joys, nor is he likely to find another occupation that will satisfy him so well, even writing novels" (240).

Shute had occasionally set short passages of a book five or ten
years in the past, but he now went back almost forty years to the
time of his own entry into aviation. His protagonist is Johnnie
Pascoe, an old pilot who had flown during World War I (this
character takes his name from a children's book written by Shute's
grandmother, Georgina Norway, entitled *Adventures of Johnnie
Pascoe* [1889]). In his earliest novels, Shute had dealt with young
Stephen Morris, who was fresh from the air war over France and who
was in many ways a portrait of his author; but Johnnie Pascoe
represented what Nevil Shute might have become had he been born
a different man. Although I in no way wish to suggest that Shute
modeled Pascoe on himself, I think it important to notice that the
author and the character were much alike in that, for the first time
since the 1930s, Shute chose a protagonist roughly his own age
(Shute was fifty-eight; Pascoe sixty); both had two daughters; both
shared certain traits such as a liking for summer packhorse trips in
the Rockies and a cautious attitude toward women: "Women liked
him, but I don't know that he liked them very much; at any rate, he
gave the impression of being careful" ([3] — this passage refers to
Pascoe, but the same thing was said to me about Shute).

The specific similarities between Shute and Pascoe are less important than the fact that Pascoe gave Shute a means of carrying himself back over a life spanning the growth of civil aviation, back to the days when he was manager of a small flying club in Yorkshire, the club where he met his own wife. Johnnie is a pilot-instructor for another provincial flying club, and falls in love with one of his students. Shute and Pascoe are also linked in history through a minor character who is a mechanic working for Pascoe in Tasmania in 1958 and who had supposedly worked for Shute's old Yorkshire club back in 1930, the year Shute met his wife. Pascoe's affair with a married woman is obviously based upon the story Shute tells in his autobiography about a pilot-instructor at the Yorkshire Aeroplane Club who had to be dismissed for similar reasons (*Slide Rule*, 61). However, the strangest connection of all between the two men is that Johnnie Pascoe dies at the age of sixty, the age at which Shute was to die. This coincidence forms another link in that chain of almost clairvoyant incidents and details that stretches throughout Shute's fiction.

Although Pascoe is the central character, he appears only in the dreams of the narrator, Ronnie Clarke. Writing to a critic, Shute referred to *The Rainbow and the Rose* as demonstrating the "flashback technique which I am developing more and more."[2] The term *flashback* was simply a convenient misnomer for the technique that Shute actually used in this novel and in such earlier novels as *An Old Captivity* and *In the Wet*. Ronnie Clarke does not have flashbacks; instead, he somehow tunes in — through "dreams" — on Pascoe's "past" existence, just as the dying man in *In the Wet* tuned in on a "future" existence. *Past* and *future* are terms that keep us from getting lost in time. In Shute's cosmos, however, a man can become lost in time under certain special conditions such as operating under stress and without sleep in a crisis that has overt or covert meaning in his life.

Shute engineered this novel's time warp with consummate skill. Ronnie Clarke, the narrator, dozing between tedious winter flights beside the radio in an airline pilots' lounge, is jerked from sleep by the news that Pascoe, the man who had taught him to fly, has crashed his small plane on a remote airstrip where he had flown to pick up a sick child. Clarke goes home and searches for his old leather coat and helmet, items he has not worn since his own early days flying in small planes. Thus he begins a trip into the past by beginning to remember things he has not thought about for thirty years. After thinking nonstop for several days about Johnnie, after

going without sleep, and after exhausting himself in Johnnie's behalf
in several unsuccessful rescue attempts, Ronnie goes to Johnnie's
empty house, drinks his whiskey, looks at his mementoes, puts on his
pajamas, sleeps in his bed, and dreams his dreams. Metaphorically,
the rising river of Ronnie Clarke's remembrance overflows the banks
of his own memory to mingle with the flood of Pascoe's.

Johnnie Pascoe's eventual death is almost obligatory; it is
demanded by the narrative method and by the fact that we come to
know so much about him. Once the narrator knows Johnnie is dead,
he flies home to suburban Melbourne and takes up his normal domestic existence. The death of one man does not matter because another
will carry his memory. Nor do the novel's adultery, illegitimacy,
suicide, and near incest make for sordidness — it may not always be
a pretty story, but it is never an ugly one.

II   *The Filming of* On the Beach

Nevil Shute's world was very orderly in these final years, as indeed
it always had been. When he was working on a new novel, he wrote
every morning without fail, sitting at the same roll-top desk he had
used since his school days. In the afternoon, he did chores around his
growing pig-and-dairy farm, or he tinkered in his machine shop.
There were constant invitations to lecture here and there, and he did
so for worthy causes, in spite of the difficulty his stutter caused him.
As his fame continued to grow, so did the endless procession of
reporters and curious readers who tried to invade his privacy.

His family and his secretary did their best to keep out interlopers,
but they could do nothing to protect him when Stanley Kramer and
a giant production unit arrived to film *On the Beach* in October,
1958. As Melbourne had no film industry, the presence of a major
motion picture company spending millions of dollars was a sensation
generating a massive public curiosity that Shute could not ignore
and that would not ignore Shute.[3] The product of his brain had
brought all those people to Melbourne, and there they were trans-
forming sections of the city into detailed simulations of what he had
imagined two or three years before in the privacy of his study.

And to the filmmaker's unintentional invasion of his emotional
privacy was added what Shute saw as an unwarranted violation of
the integrity of his book. Specifically, Stanley Kramer and John Pax-
ton, who wrote the filmscript, felt that Dwight Towers' celibacy was
unrealistic. Though there was nothing explicitly provocative or
shocking in the relationship between Towers and Moira in the

screenplay or in the completed film, a sexual relationship was definitely implied. In spite of the fact that Dwight Towers is a widower, Shute insisted that the character still regarded himself as married and that an affair with Moira would be adulterous in Towers' mind.

Shute's extreme morality extended to his characters, even when the characters were transposed from his novel to another man's film. To Kramer and to others he insisted that he had never written a story in which a married man had had an affair. Ironically, he had just finished a novel centering around an adulterous affair, but the man in that story had been divorced for many years. Besides, it took Shute over thirty years of writing to bring himself to write about adultery, and even then his internal censor was in full control: the affair happened almost thirty years before the main story opened and half a world away; the woman's husband was in a mental institution for molesting little girls — and the woman killed herself in guilt. Johnnie Pascoe had committed fornication, but that was in another country, and besides, the wench was dead.

In August, 1958, Frances Phillips, Shute's first editor at William Morrow, met him by chance in Milan. They sat down together; and, after Shute told Miss Phillips about the film underway back in Australia, she reported that "Nevil was livid. . . . I warned him he would have a heart attack if he kept on."[4] Instead of a minor heart attack like those that had plagued him for twenty years, he had a major stroke in December, 1958. In spite of its seriousness and the foretaste it gave him of his coming death, he was quickly back at work; he wrote to a friend that, apart from impaired eyesight, "the only real damage is that my face looks as though it had been kicked by a horse, but as I was no oil painting to start with this is no great matter."[5]

III Trustee from the Toolroom

At the time of Shute's stroke, he had been working on a new novel, *Trustee from the Toolroom*, for about a month; and he continued working on this novel with one eye covered by a patch to prevent double vision. His last novel, *The Rainbow and the Rose*, had carried him back thirty years to what was probably the happiest period in his life; the new novel opened on the street of his birth and presented a portrait of the house of his youth:

West Ealing is a suburb to the west of London, and Keith Stewart lives there in the lower part of No. 56 Somerset Road. No. 56 is an unusual house and a peculiarly ugly one, a detached house standing in a row but in a fairly spacious garden. . . . It was built in the spacious days of 1880 when West Ealing stood on the edge of the country farmlands and was a place to which Indian Civilians retired after their years of service. . . . The years have not dealt kindly with West Ealing; the farms are now far away. (3)

Not only does Keith Stewart live in Shute's birthplace; he is also Shute's alter ego — or one of the many portraits of his creator. Like Stewart, a professional model-engineer, Shute had his own "toolroom" (machine shop) for making scale working models of engines and other mechanical devices. An enthusiastic model engineer for many years, Shute impressed one of his brother officers during the war as a man who had never "lost the small-boy love of toys."[6] Keith Stewart writes about the models he makes for the *Miniature Mechanic*, and Shute himself was very pleased when a model engineer magazine published an article by him.

To a large extent, Shute the novelist had been a model-maker all along, creating models of reality, ideal characters and situations. There was probably a certain amount of wishful thinking on Shute's part in choosing a full-time model-maker as his protagonist, but the fact that Keith is also a writer should drive home the point that Shute is writing about someone very much like himself. And, like Shute, Stewart is a writer popular among "eccentric doctors, stockbrokers, and bank managers who just liked engineering but didn't know much about it" (4). When Shute agreed to autograph a few of his novels for a lumber magnate in Vancouver not long before he wrote *Trustee*, the lumberman produced copies of everything Shute had written — the incident gave Shute the basis for a lumber millionaire who admires Keith Stewart's work and comes unbidden to his rescue.[7]

Where the lower-middle-class Stewart differs from Shute, his upper-middle-class brother-in-law fills in the gaps. John Dermott, just mustered out of the Royal Navy at forty-five as a lieutenant commander, has the same age and rank that Shute had at the end of his naval career, and is also an avid yachtsman. Politically, Shute and Dermott are first cousins, if not blood brothers: "he held strongly right-wing views; he was a conservative in politics. He held that if a man worked hard and well and saved money he had a right to pass some of it on to his children, especially if they were girls, who usually get a raw deal anyway" (40). Dermott's concern for his daughter and his discouragement with conditions in England cause him to set out to find a new life in a new country — not Australia but British Columbia, an area that had interested Shute in the late 1950s.

Thus, Shute put his own polarity into the novel: Shute-Stewart, the modest craftsman bringing pleasure to large audiences; Norway-Dermott, the proud and restless traveler. Dermott and his wife leave their small daughter with Keith Stewart, the wife's brother, and set out to sail to their new home in Vancouver with their fortune converted to diamonds hidden in the concrete hull of their yacht in order to bypass the tight restrictions about taking currency out of England. When the yacht is driven ashore in the South Pacific in a storm and the Dermotts are drowned, Keith, the trustee of their estate, is left with the responsibility of recovering the diamonds to pay for the proper upbringing and education of his orphaned niece.

What results is the fullest statement of Shute's "travelling hopefully" theme — the story of how a little man who has never been outside of England manages to find free rides by air and sea to a small island in the Pacific in order to recover a legacy. The stroke in December and a second in May had made Shute fairly immobile. An accomplished pilot, auto racer, sailor, and horseman, an expert at all man's forms of locomotion, Shute now set the ordinarily sedentary model-maker Keith Stewart in motion while he himself stayed at home and worked on a "small four-cylinder side valve petrol motor, 30cc capacity and about 5" long. This no doubt will take me the best part of a year to build, and when it is finished I think perhaps of putting it into a small model truck fitted with radio control."[8] His letters to the Gilstraps, his friends in Oregon, are full of the joys of his workshop: "I think of all the toys that I have ever had, my workshop will be the one that stays with me to the end."[9] In effect, Shute had become his own miniature mechanic alter ego and had sent Keith Stewart to do his traveling for him.

Visiting Shute while he was working on *Trustee*, an acquaintance found a large navigation chart on his wall — Shute was not only working out the routes of his character but plotting the currents so he would have various boats at the right place at the right time.[10] These charts were more than a precaution against the few readers who might catch him in a mistake: rather, he was sailing vicariously with the Dermotts and later with Stewart. Shute, a yachtsman since his undergraduate days, had long wished to sail around the world in a small boat; his aviation work had kept him busy until World War II came; after the war, he could not resist the opportunity to fly around the world in a small plane. Though he chose his property in Australia for its proximity to good sailing, his heart trouble kept him from an extended voyage away from coastal waters.

What probably inspired him to write in *Trustee* about a difficult voyage in a small boat was the experience of his friends Miles and Beryl Smeeton, who, caught in two separate storms, had had their boat turned completely over, losing its mast each time. When Smeeton published an account of his adventures in 1959, Shute supplied the foreword and some speculations on "what might happen to a yacht overtaken by an exceptional sea while running."[11] On the near-fatal voyage described in Smeeton's book, Smeeton and his wife set out from Melbourne, leaving their young daughter behind, and also leaving in Shute's mind the question of what would happen to the child should the parents perish — a question that Shute was probably asking himself about his own daughters as his health deteriorated. As a result, he wrote a novel about a man assuming responsibility for a parentless child.

Keith Stewart's vicissitudes point to the common link between all of Shute's other "little men" — Mr. Honey, Tom Cutter, Jack Turner, the Pied Piper, the Scot pilot and slaves in *An Old Captivity* — for all of these characters undertake successful journeys that are made near-epic chiefly by the limitations of time or character. For a rich and experienced traveler to get from London to Papeete in French Oceania would be child's play; but, for the likes of Keith Stewart, such a voyage shows the giant within the little man, within all men. Such a voyage, as Shute develops his story, can be achieved only through a spider web of kindness and charity, of rewards for past favors.

After rereading *Trustee from the Toolroom*, I finally saw the relationship between Shute's prosaic style and his tremendous appeal — and the truth of a comment I had copied from a review of *Round the Bend* and pinned to my bookcase to puzzle over:

[Shute] moves at what most writers would consider an inordinately leisurely pace; he tells everything that happens, until gradually the reader is weaned away from any notion that a piling-up of details in the narrative indicates an approaching crisis in the action of the plot; he reports carefully and selectively on the towns and cities and countries his characters visit or inhabit, and describes carefully and clearly the people they meet. . . . Thus inexorably . . . he builds the idea, not of the importance of certain people, but of the importance of people in general, people good and bad, rich and poor, intelligent and stupid. And around this point of view, he weaves an atmosphere of compassion, of understanding, of perception both subjective and objective, until something very much like folk art — a myth in which a hero emerges from the people to battle for them against fate — results.[12]

Though some critics and reviewers had again and again derided the happy resolutions of his plots — what the *New Yorker* dismissed early on as "Lord Bountiful hokum" — Shute persisted until he had created "a myth in which a hero emerges from the people to battle for them": the Philip Stennings, the little men who went to war, the Mr. Honeys, the Jean Pagets, the Nigger Andersons.

And the myth was one Shute subscribed to as well. Depressed by conditions in England under the Labour government in the late 1940s, he had spent ten years writing about characters who had forsaken England. But shortly before he began *Trustee*, he told an interviewer that his gloomy forecast for England had been wrong because he had "forgotten the resilience of my own race."[13] In building his novel around a proletarian figure who does not reject the drab life that surrounds him and by shipwrecking this humble man's proud brother-in-law, Shute seems to be making amends for underrating the little man who makes the best of the world around him. The novel ends, as it begins, by looking beneath the surface of Keith Stewart: "He is one of hundreds of thousands like him in industrial England, pale faced, running to fat a little, rather hard up. His hands show evidence of manual work, his eyes and forehead evidence of intellect. . . . He has achieved the type of life that he desires; he wants no other. He is perfectly, supremely happy" (311).

IV *The Last Testaments of Nevil Shute*

When *Trustee from the Toolroom* appeared several months after Shute's death, reviewers who used this novel as a vehicle for summarizing his career found in it "a gravely joyous affirmation of the dignity and good in man in spite of his terrible periods of revolt and despair." They also discovered the message that " 'the job's the thing,' " that "a job well done makes and proclaims the man," and that there exists "the fellowship of craft and meticulous workmanship."[14] But *Trustee* was not the end, nor would Shute have wanted it read as his final testament since it was, to him, simply the book that he had found amusing to write while he was recovering from his stroke. Almost as soon as he had finished *Trustee*, he began another major novel, one of those written for himself; and he planned to write at least one other novel after that before turning to

the second stage of his autobiography, which he was already thinking of under the title "Set Square."

But his first act on finishing *Trustee* was an act of trusteeship itself:
in September, 1959, while the novel manuscript was being typed, he
began a twenty-five thousand word memorandum to Prime Minister
Menzies about the economic condition of writers and artists in
Australia. He had already given Australian writers the practical example of what could be done with Australian scenes and subject
matter for a world audience, he had helped several young Australian
writers get published outside Australia, and had lectured about the
way to success: "Accept the fact that Australia is only 4% of the
English speaking world . . . write about Australia by all means, but
write with sympathy and understanding of the other 96 per cent. Get
to know the other 96 per cent and so write about Australia in a way
that they will understand."[15] A large audience outside Australia was
essential, the speech continued, if a writer was to make enough
money to supply the leisure and freedom to develop his skills. The
memorandum to Menzies shows the same odd mixture of material
and spiritual values: unless Australian writers thrive and are
rewarded materially, then the Asian world will continue to view
Australia "as a materialistic nation devoid of spiritual values." Thus
"somehow the devotion of the Australian people to ethical principles
and spiritual values must be demonstrated to the uncommitted
nations of the world, or Australian diplomacy is not likely to cut
much ice."[16]

To Shute, the creation of a national literature was a problem to be
approached the same way a man might an engineering or financial
problem: the shortage of good writers in Australia resulted from the
profession's lack of economic support that was in turn caused by a
lack of publishing and public relations machinery for making
Australian writers internationally visible. Writers could produce a
commodity easily transportable outside the country — but what
about painters and sculptors? Shute's answer was a scheme to buy art
works for new factories and office buildings through a one percent
levy on the total construction costs. Basically anti-intellectual and
democratic, his scheme aimed at spreading patronage over the people of Australia by removing it from "the hands of the intelligentsia"
(21).

His memorandum concluded with a detailed estimate of the initial
annual cost of the proposals, thirty-five thousand pounds, and with
the practical clincher that his latest income tax bill, thirty-nine thou-

sand pounds, had been based solely upon creative writing done in Australia and upon an income derived almost exclusively outside of Australia. If, in short, one writer could provide the tax base for a national literary and artistic fund, there was no end to the possible flood of wealth such pump-priming could bring.

Shute must have known his time was running out and that the effort required for the lengthy and detailed memorandum might better have been spent on a new novel. But, since he had lived well by writing, he wished to pass on what he had learned and to see his wealth used to create more wealth and more pleasurable art. The memorandum to Menzies was, then, just one act of a man who was putting his own life in order and who had been doing so for several years. He had made his older daughter his secretary and had taken her on several visits to his publishers and agents in England and America to assure a knowledgeable executrix of his literary estate. His writing had brought him a large steady income and a responsibility to dispose of it fittingly, as in his gift of eight thousand pounds for building a new church in Langwarrin. "He took trouble to think out how his generosity could best be used," wrote Shute's old Shrewsbury housemaster. "And there was nothing patronizing about it..... he would visit aged relations and tell them that, as they were not comfortably housed, he had bought a house for them. . . . he helped to make possible, by an outright gift to the publishers, the publication of an expensive specialist book by a friend."[17]

The care exhibited by the trustee from the toolroom in recovering a lost legacy showed itself in Shute's care for his family — in April, 1958, he wrote a will even more complicated than the one in *A Town Like Alice* to guarantee his wife and daughters a permanent income; and he directed that the income from his estate should go, on the deaths of his immediate heirs, to his old schools, Balliol and Shrewsbury, with the "wish that this money be employed at their discretion for the benefit of students from the Commonwealth and especially from Australia."

V *Begins Last Novel*

In November, Shute began the actual writing of a major novel that had been on his mind for some time: "Incident at Eucla." The manuscript notes indicate that the first stage of his thinking was a play to be called "Nativity at Eucla" and that it was to deal with the miraculous birth of a baby at a deserted telegraph station on the barren southern coast of Australia. It is hard to say whether the first few pages of notes indicate Shute was going back over the path that led him to *Beyond the Black Stump* and *On the Beach* or whether his notes themselves were written before those two novels. The setting of the new novel is an area that Shute had visited by car in preparation for *Beyond the Black Stump* (the narrator drives the same kind of station wagon as Shute); and the characters are a reunion of the cast for the two earlier novels: an Australian farm girl, an English boy, an American oil geologist, an Australian scientist.

After two pages of notes for the dramatic version, Shute shifted to notes for a novel in which "three wise men" assemble by chance (or is it by divine plan?) and bring a series of gifts that sound like a return to the wishful thinking that had preceded the writing of *On the Beach:*

1. Gift of oil to Australia through known coal.
2. Gift of water by magnetic distillation. . . .
3. Defense against radioactivity.[18]

In other words, self-sufficiency in industry and in agriculture were to be combined with protection from the follies of the rest of the world; and both were to be sanctified through an implied or explicit Second Coming in the form of child born in a "great barnlike stone building" among sheep, pigs, and a prize bull to a half-caste couple named Joe and Daydream Mary. Joe, naturally, is a carpenter's helper; and the other Christian paraphernalia in the notes and in the thirty pages of typescript is equally obligatory: for example, a nativity star in the form of a satellite is expected by the wise man from Princeton.

Shute had used the Australian nativity motif to lend symbolic weight to his Commonwealth predictions in *In the Wet.* And, while he was preparing to write the messianic *Round the Bend*, he had sneaked a baby named *Noel* into *A Town Like Alice* — Noel was Jean Paget's child by Joe, the man who survived crucifixion. The nativity in "Incident at Eucla" was probably meant to be a metaphorical framework rather than the subject of the novel; things were to happen because of the birth — or was the birth itself a response to what was happening in the world? In any case, all the notes return to the theme of nuclear research; and they seem to point to some resolution that would benefit Australia alone. In short, Shute seems to have put aside the universal vision that had given *On the Beach* its power.

But the difference between the bare framework of Shute's notes and the actual novel was always great. "Incident at Eucla" starts with a chapter reflected in the notes, a chapter that seems particularly personal to Shute. William Spear, the narrator, is an engineer the same age as Shute, but his wife seems an even closer self-portrait: an Oxford graduate, her bookcase contains Shute's own personal favorites: "She had loved William Morris and, indeed, all the Pre-Raphaelites; there was *The Wood Beyond the World*, and *The Water of the Wondrous Isles* and *The Earthly Paradise . . . Oxford Poetry* was there in many little paper covered volumes." Only two months before he died, Shute opened "Eucla" with the death of Mrs. Spear and with Spear's decision to go to Australia to put a plaque reading "Let us remember them who have died for us" on the grave of his only child, a meteorologist killed in a plane crash during World War II. As in *Requiem for a Wren*, *The Rainbow and the Rose*, *Trustee from the Toolroom*, and *On the Beach*, we have a man picking up the pieces after death or disaster. It was almost as though Shute was denying his own mortality by having others die, by escaping back over the very road along the southern Australian coast he had traveled five years before, by journeying into that psychic wilderness that had intrigued him ever since *An Old Captivity*.

The writing of "Incident at Eucla" progressed well through November and December though Shute was kept busy with other concerns: a private preview of *On the Beach* ("the worst film that has ever been made of one of my books, without exception," he wrote Dr. Gilstrap; "I am drafting a statement for the Press with my solicitor which shall not be actionable"[19]); negotiations for a film of *Round the Bend;* and getting in the hay for his livestock before Christmas. The new year came and passed, and he settled into his book. On January 11, he took the time to write a friendly letter to David Martin, a novelist who was writing an article about him for the prestigious quarterly *Meanjin*. The once neat signature drops away, downhill, the mark of a man whose body is not responding properly. The next morning, January 12, he went into his small study and sat at the typewriter. The last sentence he wrote reads: "There was a fluffy haired young girl with them, helping somewhat ineffectually and she was weeping, the tears running quietly down her cheeks." He fell ill; an ambulance was called about noon; and he lapsed into a coma as it sped to the hospital. He died that evening without recovering consciousness, but his last memory was one of traveling.

CHAPTER 12

Setting Square

" "TO travel hopefully is a better thing than to arrive, and the true success is to labour" — Nevil Shute took these words from Robert Louis Stevenson as the epigraph for his autobiography,. *Slide Rule*, which he originally intended to call "The True Success." Though travel, movement, is his key metaphor, Shute's own true success came to more than traveling or laboring: he arrived when others failed. Things worked out well for Nevil Shute. Even his death came quickly and without awareness or drama: his twenty-third book was at the publisher's; his twenty-fourth was in the typewriter; and a film based on his most famous novel, *On the Beach*, was showing in movie houses around the world.

Shute's obituaries invariably stressed his phenomenal popularity: "no other English writer of his day approached the combined sales in England of novels that he turned out year after year"; he was the "top bestseller of all contemporary British authors."[1] His annual income from royalties was respectfully reported as being one hundred and seventy-five thousand dollars. At the time of his death (and a few months later, when *Trustee from the Toolroom* appeared) there were many attempts to explain why Shute had stayed at the top of the best-seller lists for over two decades. A typical explanation appeared in the *Saturday Review:* "[*Trustee*] is sentimental but safely short of repulsiveness, celebrating a self-reliance that asks few favors and ends by having large favors thrust upon it. It is a fable, a happy story in which virtues are handsomely rewarded."[2]

Today, nearly two decades after Shute's death, all of his novels are still in print. Why do people still read Nevil Shute? One answer is implied in a popular guide to world literature: "All Shute's novels have a high moral purpose and happy endings, and are written in an easy style which practically reads itself."[3] Actually, not all of the endings are happy, though Shute's novels do tend to leave the impression that things have turned out (or will turn out) for the best. But the other two points are well-taken. For one, Shute's books are appealing to readers who seek gently delivered moral "instruction." Incapable of telling a "low" story, or one in which his obvious sincerity did not shine through, Nevil Shute was a master of the middle-class story: the story of well-meaning and honest men and women reaching for success that can be measured in terms of money, victory over an opponent, happiness, love, personal fulfillment, or self-understanding. Secondly, Shute was equally the master of a clear and simple style. In spite of his obvious weaknesses — wooden characters, reliance on certain stock situations, and other common faults of the prolific popular writer — Shute never failed to find the proper words and tone to take the readers into his confidence and hold them there. His prose was never exciting, nor was it ever dull: it was simply as functional as the aircraft he built in his engineering days.

Shute was, in the words of the current *Encyclopaedia Britannica,* a "novelist who showed a special talent for weaving his technical knowledge of engineering into the texture of his fiction narrative."[4] This talent helped him reach the upper limits of popular success because it gave his fiction a highly realistic and believable quality. But this talent would have been worthless were Shute not involved with his world. Ultimately, Shute was successful because he strove to interpret the world he knew to the common reader. At first he wrote about his own profession and interests (the aviation industry and flying) in such a way as to capture and educate an ever-widening audience. Then he expanded his subject matter to help Britain prepare for its struggle in World War II. Finally, he began to take English readers with him beyond their island, introducing them — and millions of Americans — to Australia.

Throughout his career, his one great message was that of the need for understanding, for a posture of openness to the possibilities of life. In his best novels, he demanded of his readers that they accept the outer limits of the human mind's potential (the mental journeys in *An Old Captivity, No Highway,* and *In the Wet*). He demanded that his readers — mostly white Protestants — open their own minds to accept characters who differed from them in race and belief (*The Chequer Board* and *Round the Bend*). He demanded that his readers look to the future and see with him its dangers — of strategic bombing (*What Happened to the Corbetts*), of the decline of England's strength (*In the Wet*), of nuclear holocaust (*On the Beach*).

If Nevil Shute ever influenced another writer or the course of English literature, there is no evidence to that effect. Nor is his influence on his huge audience measurable. People still read Shute, but they do not, as my bibliography shows, write much about him. There is little formal criticism of Shute: several articles, an introduction to a special edition of his works, a number of extended reviews. In surveys of the modern novel or of English literature, Shute is either ignored entirely, pushed into footnotes, or explicitly excluded from consideration (as at both the beginning and the end of Anthony Burgess' *The Novel Now*[5]). But Shute has his partisans, chiefly C. P. Snow, who found him a bridge between the two cultures[6] — an engineer who could speak to the general reader as well as to professionals. Shute's great value, I think, is that like Albert Camus' Tarrou (in *The Plague*), he "had a habit of observing events and people through the wrong end of a telescope. In those chaotic times he set himself to recording the history of what the normal historian passes over."[7] To end my study, I would like to cite the final assessment of Shute by one of the major organs of popular history, *Time* magazine: "later years may find [his novels] a remarkably reliable portrait of mid-20th century man and his concerns."[8]

Notes and References

In citations from unpublished letters and manuscripts, "Syracuse" refers to microfilm on deposit in the Syracuse University Library; "Heinemann" and "Morrow" refer to the files of these publishers. Letters not otherwise identified by place of deposit are usually in possession of the addressee.

Preface

1. "Shute Shoots Back," *Books and Bookmen* (September, 1958), p. 11.
2. Ibid.

Chapter One

1. With two exceptions, page numbers for quotations from Nevil Shute's published works documented directly in the text refer to the original American editions published by William Morrow and listed in the bibliography; quotations from *Marazan* and *So Disdained*, not published by Morrow, are taken from the Uniform Edition first issued in 1951 by William Heinemann, Shute's British publisher.
2. "A Memorandum about Creative Writers, Artists, and Composers in Australia" (Manuscript Series 3/3).
3. Here and elsewhere I base references to specific dates for compostion on those Shute marked on his manuscripts.
4. Shute to publisher, September 3, 1923, Manuscript Series 2/22.
5. J. B. Pettigrew, "Flight," in *Encyclopaedia Britannica* (1879); IX, 323.
6. Alan Cobham, *Skyways* (London, 1925), p. 304.

Chapter Two

1. In addition to Shute's autobiography, *Slide Rule*, which deals with the R. 100, see James Leasor's *The Millionth Chance* (New York 1957), which deals with the R.101.
2. Kipling's lines are used as the epigraph and are quoted directly by Stenning on page 37.
3. See Shute's introduction to the Heinemann Uniform Editions of *Marazan, So Disdained*, and *Lonely Road*.
4. Cobham, *Skyways*, p. vi.

5. "The Airship Venture," *Blackwood's Magazine* (May, 1933), p. 627; later incorporated into *Slide Rule*.

6. Ibid.

Chapter Three

1. William Buchan in his general introduction to the Heron Edition of Shute's works (London, n.d.), p. 4.

2. Quoted from a reader's report in the Morrow files.

3. Flora Twort to Julian Smith, 1970.

4. See "The Airship Venture" and "Air Circus," *Blackwood's Magazine* (October, 1937), pp. 433 - 72.

5. David Martin, "The Mind That Conceived *On the Beach*," *Meanjin* 19 (June, 1960), 197.

6. Anon., "Briefly Noted," *New Yorker*, May 28, 1938, p. 63.

7. Anon., "New Books: A Reader's List," *New Republic*, June 15, 1938, p. 168.

8. Roger Burlingame, "Haunting Modern Fairy Tale," *New York Herald Tribune Books*, May 29, 1938, p. 2.

9. Anon., "Books and Authors," *New York Times Book Review*, April 17, 1938, p. 14.

10. Sydney Hansel to Julian Smith, 1970.

Chapter Four

1. Quoted by John K. Hutchens, "Nevil Shute," *New York Herald Tribune Book Review*, September 14, 1952, p. 2.

2. "Shute Shoots Back," p. 11.

3. Untitled, unpublished essay on the writing of *Slide Rule* (Syracuse).

4. André Maurois, "Splendide Isolement," *Les Annales Politiques et Litteraires* 114 (September 25, 1939), 308 - 9.

5. "The Young Captives," *Wings: The Literary Guild Magazine* (March, 1940), p. 5.

6. See "Knightly Vigil" (Manuscript Series 1/2).

7. Fridtjof Nansen, *In Northern Mists* (New York, 1911).

8. "The Young Captives," p. 8.

9. Fred T. Marsh, "The Story of a Strange Flight," *New York Times Book Review*, February 25, 1940, p. 6.

10. I am grateful to Sydney Hansel for information about Shute's work with Burney (letter, 1970).

11. "Drama in the R.A.F.," *Times Literary Supplement*, November 23, 1940, p. 589.

12. George Orwell, "New Novels," *New Statesman and Nation*, December 7, 1940, p. 574.

Chapter Five

1. Gerald Pawle, *The Secret War* (New York, 1957), p. 35.

2. Shute in his preface to *The Secret War*, p. 5.

3. Shute quoted in a press release for *The Chequer Board* (Morrow files).

4. Pawle, p. 119.

5. The German measles story is reported by Pawle, p. 119; since Pawle incorporated a lengthy memoir by Shute in his book, this detail may have come directly from Shute.

6. Sir Charles Goodeve to Julian Smith, 1970.

7. Edward Weeks, "The Atlantic Bookshelf," *Atlantic* (February, 1942), n.p.

8. Quoted by Hutchens, "Nevil Shute," p. 2.

9. Pawle, p. 178.

10. Edward Terrell, *Admiralty Brief: The Story of Inventions That Contributed to Victory in the Battle of the Atlantic* (London, 1958), p. 40.

11. Pawle, p. 56.

12. Ibid., p. 42.

13. Shute to David Martin, January 11, 1960.

14. Anon., "Briefly Noted," *New Yorker*, October 20, 1945, p. 112.

15. Flora Twort to Julian Smith, 1970.

16. Shute to David Martin, January 11, 1960.

17. Shute to Dwye Evans, January 13, 1943 (Heinemann files).

18. Pawle to Julian Smith, letter and interview, 1970. Another former member of the Department of Miscellaneous Weapon Development, Alec Menhinick, wrote me in 1971 that Shute sent a very angry and critical letter to a senior admiral concerning the censorship of *Most Secret;* in Menhinick's opinion, Shute's later transfer to the Ministry of Information was a result of this letter.

19. Sydney Hansel to Julian Smith, 1970.

20. Shute's letter to Pawle is dated July 12, 1954.

21. Shute's letter, dated June 21, 1945, is in Manuscript Series 1/4.

22. Edward Weeks, "The Atlantic Bookshelf," *Atlantic*, August, 1944, p. 125.

23. *The Second Front*, Manuscript Series 1/3.

24. Anon., "Love in Strife," *Times Literary Supplement*, September 23, 1944, p. 461.

Chapter Six

1. A Summary of Shute's literary income is given in his "Memorandum about Creative Writers . . . in Australia," p. 11.

2. "What Went into *The Chequer Board*," *Wings: The Literary Guild Review*, April, 1947, p. 6.

3. Walter White, *A Rising Wind* (Garden City, 1945).

4. Thomas Sugrue, "The Post-War Re-Education of a Briton," *New York Herald Tribune Weekly Book Review*, March 30, 1947, p. 1.

5. "On Stirring Up Hornets Nests," undated notes for a speech (Syracuse).

6. Shute to David Martin, January 11, 1960.

7. Quoted by Walter White in an editorial in the *Chicago Defender*, March 29, 1947, p. 15.

8. *New Statesman and Nation*, July 26, 1947, p. 71.

9. "Heavier-than-air Craft," in Charles Dennistoun Burney's *The World, the Air and the Future* (London, 1929), p. 279.

10. P. B. Walker, "Fatigue of Aircraft Structures," *The Journal of the Royal Aeronautical Society* 53 (1949), 763 - 78.

Chapter Seven

1. Pamela Hansford Johnson, "New Novels," *New Statesman*, August 16, 1958, p. 200.

2. Mrs. Norway in an interview with Julian Smith, 1970.

3. The story (ca. 1925) and the scenario (ca. 1948) are in Manuscript Series 1/2 and 3/1.

4. Heather Mayfield to Julian Smith, 1970.

5. William Blake, "Preface" to *Milton*, in *Blake: Complete Writings*, ed. Geoffrey Keynes (London, 1966), pp. 480 - 81.

6. "A Memorandum about Creative Writers . . . ," p. 13.

7. Shute to Gerald Pawle, July 12, 1954.

8. James Riddell in an interview with Julian Smith, 1970.

9. Flight log entry for October 25, 1948; James Riddell reports this prophecy in almost the same words in *Flight of Fancy* (New York, 1951), p. 72.

10. "Shute Shoots Back," p. 11.

11. William Buchan in his general introduction to the Heron Edition, p. 12.

12. Mrs. C. L. Gilstrap to Julian Smith, 1971; the pilot was her son.

13. James Riddell, *Flight of Fancy*, pp. 209, 245.

14. Edward Weeks, "The Atlantic Bookshelf," *Atlantic*, March, 1951, p. 79.

15. Edward Gray, "Exploring Holy Ground," *Saturday Review*, March 17, 1951, p. 28.

Chapter Eight

1. Sally Bessant to Julian Smith, July 21, 1970.

2. "My Week," an unpublished biographical sketch written early in 1950 (Syracuse).

3. Sally Bessant to Julian Smith, July 21, 1970.

4. Paul Farrell, "Books," *Commonweal*, June 30, 1950, p. 301.

5. Anon., "Too Good to Be True," *Time*, June 12, 1950, p. 102.

6. Anon., "Danger Abroad," *Times Literary Supplement*, June 16, 1950, p. 369.

7. Shute to David Martin, January 11, 1960.

8. In an interview with Betty Lee ("Nevil Shute: He Believes the World Will Survive After All" [Toronto] *Globe Magazine*, February 21, 1959, p. 12).

9. William Buchan in general introduction to the Heron Edition of Shute's works, p. 9.

10. In an interview with Robert Pitman, the London *Sunday Express*, May 14, 1961.

11. Speech before Royal Empire Society, October 9, 1952 (Syracuse).

Chapter Nine

1. Quoted by Betty Lee in her Toronto *Globe Magazine* interview, February 21, 1959, p. 12.

2. Shute to Betty Vaughan, March 3, 1952 (Morrow files).

3. These figures are from his "Memorandum about Creative Writers," pp. 11 - 12, 50.

4. Arnold Gyde to Shute, May 31, 1951 (Heinemann files).

5. Unpublished exhibition lecture notes, April 30, 1951 (Syracuse).

6. "Memorandum," p. 12.

7. Unpublished speech notes, October 10, 1951 (Syracuse).

8. Shute to David Martin, January 11, 1960; italics mine.

9. According to several clippings in the Morrow files, the location Shute chose for a future royal residence was later selected by the Australian government.

10. The manuscript is dated November 25, 1951, to May 25, 1952.

11. Shute to Dwye Evans, September 4, 1952 (Heinemann files).

12. From a hymn written by C. A. Alington, headmaster of Shrewsbury School in Shute's days there.

13. Draft of speech before Victoria League, October 7, 1952 (Syracuse). An expanded version of this speech and of his speech of October 9, 1952, before the Royal Empire Society was later published as *The Future Population of Australia*, a pamphlet prepared for the Australian Citizenship Convention (Canberra, 1959).

14. Anon., "Authors Changing Public Opinion," London *Times*, July 22, 1960, p. 4.

15. Robert Greacen, "Social Class in Post-War English Fiction," *Southern Review* 4 (1968), 151.

16. Place and exact date of this unpublished speech are unknown, but probably very soon after publication of *In the Wet* in mid-1953 (Syracuse).

17. Shute to R. P. Watt, January 15, 1954 (Heinemann files).

18. Shute to Gerald Pawle, July 12, 1954.

19. "Shute Shoots Back," p. 11.

20. Unpublished speech notes, October 10, 1951 (Syracuse).

Chapter Ten

1. Unpublished speech of October 7, 1952 (Syracuse).

2. Shute quoted from memory by his friend Jeannie Scott in a letter to Mrs. C. L. Gilstrap; though the quotation is second hand, Heather Mayfield, Shute's daughter, has vouched for its accuracy.

3. Shute to Ward Cannel of the Newspaper Enterprise Association Service, ca. September, 1957 (Morrow files).

4. Shute to Dr. Gilstrap, July 16, 1954.

5. Shute to Mrs. Gilstrap, September 20, 1954.

6. The idea of flying a jet slightly above track level at night toward a train to frighten the engineer into thinking another train is coming was not pure imagination: Shute heard such a story from the Gilstraps' pilot son (Mrs. C. L. Gilstrap to Julian Smith, 1971).

7. In an unpublished interview with Rochelle Girson, June, 1953 (Morrow files).

8. Untitled, undated manuscript on the writing of *Slide Rule* (Syracuse).

9. Burney quoted in his *New York Times* obituary, November 13, 1968, p. 47.

10. Shute quoted by Dwye Evans in a memo, January 18, 1957 (Heinemann files).

11. See Milgram's "Behavioral Study of Obedience," *Journal of Abnormal and Social Psychology* 67 (October, 1963), 371 - 78.

12. Colin Young, "Nobody Dies," in *Film: Book 2*, ed. Robert Hughes (New York 1962), p. 92.

13. David Martin, "The Mind That Conceived *On the Beach*," p. 194.

14. Shute to Martin, January 11, 1960.

15. Ibid.

16. Philip Wylie to Shute's American publishers, June 19, 1957 (Morrow files).

Chapter Eleven

1. Shute to Gerald Pawle, April, 1956.

2. Shute to David Martin, January 11, 1960.

3. For Stanley Kramer's impact on the Melbourne area, see John H. Valder, "On a Moviemaking Cook's Tour 'Down Under,' " *New York Times*, March 8, 1959, II, 7.

4. Frances Phillips in an interview with Julian Smith, 1970.

5. Shute to Dr. Gilstrap, January 5, 1959.

6. Terrell, *Admiralty Brief*, p. 39.

7. Sydney Hansel to Julian Smith, 1970.

8. Shute to Dr. Gilstrap, April 17, 1959.

9. Shute to Dr. Gilstrap, June 22, 1959.

10. Theo Sambell in an interview with Julian Smith, 1970.

11. In Miles Smeeton, *Once is Enough* (New York, 1959), p. 203.

12. Thomas Sugrue, "Mr. Shute, Again Casual and Exciting," *New York Herald Tribune Book Review*, March 4, 1951, p. 4.

13. Shute quoted by Charles Curran in letter to London *Times*, July 29, 1960, p. 11.

14. "Off the Beach," *Times Literary Supplement*, April 1, 1960, p. 213; "Hero Minus Heroics," *Time*, April 4, 1960, p. 94; Edmund Fuller, "Last Tale of a Skilled Storyteller," *Saturday Review*, April 2, 1960, p. 17 (on the cover of this issue is probably the best published photograph of Shute).

15. Unpublished speech before writers' convention at Seaford, November, 1957 (Syracuse).

16. "Memorandum about Creative Writers . . . ," pp. 1 - 2.

17. "J.B.O." in a letter to the London *Times*, January 28, 1960, p. 16.

18. Manuscript Series 1/1 contains eight pages of detailed longhand notes and thirty pages of single-spaced typescript.

19. Shute to Dr. Gilstrap, December 10, 1959.

Chapter Twelve

1. Anon., "Nevil Shute Dies," *New York Times*, January 13, 1960, p. 47; anon., "The Two Lives of Nevil Shute," *Time*, January 25, 1960, p. 94.

2. Fuller, "Last Tale of a Skilled Storyteller," p. 16.

3. J[an] M[arsh], "Nevil Shute," in *The Penguin Companion to English Literature*, ed. David Daiches (New York, 1971), pp. 476 - 77.

4. Anon., "Nevil Shute," *Encylopaedia Britannica* (1974), IX, 175.

5. Anthony Burgess, *The Novel Now* (New York, 1967), pp. 20, 206.

6. C. P. Snow to Julian Smith, 1970.

7. Albert Camus, *The Plague* (New York, 1948), p. 22.

8. Anon., "Two Lives of Nevil Shute," p. 94.

Selected Bibliography

PRIMARY SOURCES

1. Books (American titles are given in parentheses.)

Marazan. London: Cassell, 1926; reissued London: Heinemann, 1951.

So Disdained (The Mysterious Aviator). London: Cassell, 1928; Boston: Houghton Mifflin, 1928; reissued London: Heinemann, 1951.

Lonely Road. London: Cassell, 1932; New York: Morrow, 1932; reissued London: Heinemann, 1951.

Ruined City (Kindling). London: Heinemann, 1938; New York: Morrow, 1938.

What Happened to the Corbetts (Ordeal). London: Heinemann, 1939; New York: Morrow, 1939.

An Old Captivity. London: Heinemann, 1940; New York: Morrow, 1940.

Landfall: A Channel Story. London: Heinemann, 1940; New York: Morrow, 1940.

Pied Piper. London: Heinemann, 1942; New York: Morrow, 1942.

Pastoral. London: Heinemann, 1944; New York: Morrow, 1944.

Most Secret. London: Heinemann, 1945; New York: Morrow, 1945.

Vinland the Good. London: Heinemann, 1946; New York: Morrow, 1946.

The Chequer Board. London: Heinemann, 1947; New York: Morrow, 1947.

No Highway. London: Heinemann, 1948; New York: Morrow, 1948.

A Town Like Alice (The Legacy). London: Heinemann, 1950; New York: Morrow, 1950.

Round the Bend. London: Heinemann, 1951; New York: Morrow, 1951.

The Far Country. London: Heinemann, 1952; New York: Morrow, 1952.

In the Wet. London: Heinemann, 1953; New York: Morrow, 1953.

Slide Rule; The Autobiography of an Engineer. London: Heinemann, 1954; New York: Morrow, 1954.

Requiem for a Wren (The Breaking Wave). London: Heinemann, 1955; New York: Morrow, 1955.

Beyond the Black Stump. London: Heinemann, 1956; New York; Morrow, 1956.

On the Beach. London: Heinemann, 1957; New York: Morrow, 1957.

The Rainbow and the Rose. London: Heinemann, 1958; New York: Morrow, 1958.
Trustee from the Toolroom. London: Heinemann, 1960; New York: Morrow, 1960.
Stephen Morris. London: Heinemann, 1961; New York: Morrow, 1961.

2. Manuscripts
All of Shute's extant manuscripts (some four dozen items) are in the National Library of Australia. Microfilm copies of these manuscripts are available at the Arents Library of Syracuse University. As a detailed "preliminary calendar" of the Syracuse microfilm holdings is available (see Applegate article in *Secondary Sources,* below), this list is confined to major items.
a. Series 1: Unpublished Manuscripts
"Incident at Eucla": thirty-page typescript, dated November 15, 1959, of the first two and a half chapters of the novel Shute was working on at the time of his death. Eight pages of manuscript notes outline the plot and character development (Series 1/Item 1).
Short Stories, Articles, and Fragments: seven items dating from about 1923 (1/2a - g).
Ministry of Information Sketches and Correspondence: about a dozen articles written during World War II for the British Ministry of Information; roughly half deal with preparations for the Normandy Invasion; the other half deal with Shute's travels in Burma late in the war (1/3a - d; 1/4a - g).
"The Lame Ducks Fly": twenty-page typescript, undated, of the first chapter of the unfinished novel Shute began just before *Landfall* (1/5).
"The Seafarers": two typescript versions, undated, of a novella written right after World War II (1/6a - b).
"Blind Understanding": one hundred and twenty-three page typescript, dated March 8, 1948, of an unfinished novel about a former Wren (1/7).
"Pastoral": ninety-page typescript, undated, of a film scenario based on Shute's novel of the same title (1/8).

b. Series 2: Published Material
Contains manuscripts (typed) for all of Shute's books except for *Marazan, So Disdained,* and *Lonely Road;* most typescripts contain a great number of Shute's holograph additions and corrections as well as Shute's notes on names, titles, plot development, setting, characterization, and chronology. Also contains undated typescripts for the article "The Airship Venture" (2/6) and the story "Air Circus" (2/21), two minor pieces published in *Blackwood's Magazine* in May, 1933, and October 1937. Applegate's article (below) gives a detailed description of each manuscript.

c. Series 3: Other Manuscripts
Contains four unpublished items, including:

"A Memorandum about Creative Writers, Artists, and Composers in Australia": fifty-page typescript of a report submitted to Prime Minister Menzies on October 20, 1959 (3/3).

"Flight Log from England to Australia": one hundred and ninety-six page typescript of letters Shute sent home during his round trip between England and Australia; covers events from September 22, 1948, to March 14, 1949 (3/4).

SECONDARY SOURCES

Criticism of Shute's fiction is limited almost entirely to hundreds of major reviews, the best of which appeared in the *Times Literary Supplement*, the *New York Times*, the *New York Herald Tribune*, and the *Saturday Review*. As I have already cited many representative reviews in "Notes and References," I have limited this brief list to only the most helpful items.

APPLEGATE, HOWARD L. "Preliminary Calendar of the Nevil Shute Norway Manuscripts Microfilm." *The Courier* 9 (October, 1971), 14 - 20. Lists and describes Shute's manuscripts for published and unpublished works in the Syracuse University Library collection.

MARTIN, DAVID. "The Mind that Conceived *On the Beach*." *Meanjin* 19 (June, 1960), 193 - 200. Sensitive analysis of Shute's importance.

NORWAY, MRS. HAMILTON. *The Sinn Fein Rebellion as I Saw It*. London: Smith, Elder and Company, 1916. Interesting for glimpses of Shute as a youth of seventeen during a period of crisis.

PAWLE, GERALD. *The Secret War*. New York: W. Sloane Associates, 1957. This book, with an introduction by Shute, is valuable for its glimpses of Shute as an engineer and administrator during World War II.

RIDDELL, JAMES. *Flight of Fancy*. New York: Duell, Sloane and Pearce, 1951. Contains an introduction by Shute; an account of traveling across Asia and Australia with him.

SMITH, JULIAN. "In Search of Nevil Shute." *The Courier* 9 (October, 1971), 8 - 13. Bibliographical survey of Shute's publications and manuscripts; some comments on secondary sources.

TAYLOR, H. A. *Airspeed Aircraft Since 1931*. London: Putnam, 1970. Deals with the company Shute helped found and direct.

Index